Secrets of the Land

Designing Harmonious Gardens with Feng Shui

Shelley Sparks

Published by Harmony Gardens Unlimited
12224 Addison Street
Valley Village, CA 91607
818-505-9783
http://www.harmonygardens.net

Book Design and Cover by Book Studio/Rosamond Grupp
Edited by Christine LePorte, Jeanne McCafferty and Davida Rappaport

Secrets of the Land: Secrets of the Land offers countless ways to learn about your garden. It encourages people to plan your own garden by teaching the basics of design, the basis for feng shui, and how to use the tools of plants, colors, rocks and water to implement your design. Secrets of the Land is packed with accessible information to blend the unfamiliar with down to earth recommendations for designing your garden beautifully.

ISBN-13: 978-0-9839552-6-9

ISBN-10: 0983955263

Contents

Foreword

His Holiness Grandmaster Lin Yun, Rinpoche

Shelley Sparks uses different lines of vision and different angles to look at the garden, adding to it what Eastern philosophy emphasizes: Feng Shui. What's more, she also includes intuition which stems from spiritual studies, which surpasses just looking at gardens from the surface. Since intuition is abstract, it can enhance the spirituality of the garden in terms of feng shui. When the "Theory of Ch'i", which I have established is applied throughout the design of gardens, the harmony of Yin and Yang would bring about an invisible force of spiritual power. Shelley Sparks infuses the Five Elements, the Bagua and the Yin and Yang of the Tai chi into garden design and utilizes the most secretive of secret transcendental solutions as a means to fix or strengthen the design. Any problem or trouble area with garden design can be resolved with ease so that your sensibility could be understood through the garden. From the garden, you could see deeper and more meaningful aspects of the ancient Eastern cultures and you will know that your garden design is the innovative product which combines the wisdom of Confucianism, Taoism, Buddhism and Tantric Buddhism. You will know how to highlight the specialties of different plants and how to arrange the plants according to their color so that the feature and the significance of the garden would be well presented in layers and stages.

The garden affects our everyday life, our families and our societies, therefore the best garden design should contain nine methods of transcendental solutions such as paying attention to the Three Secret Reinforcement and features of Ch'i.

In this universe there are three kinds of energies: one from the heaven, one from the earth and one from humans. In this book Shelley Sparks has analyzed this very clearly. As for the harmony of the Yin-Yang in the garden, Eastern gardens tend to use rocks and water to represent the Yin and Yan, since they represent the relative relationship of hardness and softness. Therefore the selection and arrangement of rocks and water is worthy of clear and lengthy discussion as presented by Shelley Sparks. I would suggest you read it carefully because in no other publication would you find such information, because Shelley Sparks has a wonderful mind, very sharp wisdom and superb viewpoints.

She is especially knowledgeable about the Five Elements, Bagua and Yin-Yang and how to apply them to the harmony within the house and the garden. Using feng shui to adjust both the interior and exterior of the house is also a form of invisible knowledge. In the garden, Shelley Sparks has already formed an abstract Bagua in her heart and superimposed it onto the garden so that she would know the various Bagua positions that need to be accentuated so that the owner of the house would enjoy success or gain unexpected happiness or reasons for celebration. For example, planting peach blossoms in Kan, the Marriage position, would enable the family's single daughter who cannot find an ideal mate to walk down the aisle in the near future. Another example would be planting a pomegranate tree in the Tui, the Children position of the garden so that parents who are hoping to have a child will soon have a pregnancy. It is important to know what kinds of flowers and what kind of trees should be planted at which Bagua position. If small birds such as orioles or mynas are going to be kept in the garden, then their cages should be hung on the branches of certain trees.

As for the shape of the garden and how to use roads or other buildings to strengthen the reference and relationship with the house, these are also discussed in this book. The placement of ponds, greenhouse, sewage system, principles for placing lights and water pipes are all detailed very clearly in this book.

Shelley Sparks begins with her visualization when she designs concepts from the design of the house to the placement of the garden. She is especially knowledgeable about the abstract spiritual studies and the subtle and not always detectable Zen. She clearly explains the most secretive of secret transcendental solutions, and how to proceed with a blessing ceremony so that the readers could readily understand. She also thoroughly provides details about the most secretive of secret transcendental solutions, including the use of cinnabar rice and orange peels.

Shelley Sparks very sincerely teaches the readers how to rid any evil Ch'i from the foundation of the house to the creating of a garden. She also includes very powerful transcendental solutions such as the Auspicious Light Flags, the Placement of the Eight Doors and how to pay respect to the Earth God and the Mountain God. Therefore, this book is a fantastic work that will surely be read throughout the ages and its value cannot be examined with average judgment criteria. This is because Shelley Sparks is always ready to add in new thoughts and new concepts bridged with modern lifestyle and modern science, so that her readers will be able to enter a better life. This is the supreme value of this book which cannot be seen with the naked eye.

The ancients say, "One good deed averts a thousand evils." When Shelley Sparks wrote this book, she has performed more than just one good deed; she has done tens and hundreds of good deeds. She has accumulated a lot of merits and good karma, and helped so many people who needed to be helped. Therefore, the good effects, good karma, will be limitless for the rest of her life.

Lin Yun,
January 17, 2010

Foreword

H.H. Khadro Crystal Chu Rinpoche
Spiritual Leader of Black Sect Buddhism at Fifth Stage
CEO of Yun Lin Temple

I am extremely pleased to see that another book has come out based on Black Sect Tantric Buddhist Feng Shui theories which were developed and taught by late His Holiness Grandmaster Professor Lin Yun, our much beloved and highly respected teacher.

A designed garden is a piece of artwork. It not only provides beautiful scenery, but also brings to mind creativity, depth of philosophy, diversity of cultures, passion for aesthetic, and even a touch of spirituality. In a well-designed landscape, one can see dynamic movement in static serenity, as well as feel soothing softness in enchanted strength.

This book is not just an ordinary book about garden design. Instead it incorporates the ideologies, principles, methods, and applications of Feng Shui into landscaping which makes the book very special and instrumental. It opens up an entire different perspective to designing a garden. The author, Shelley Sparks, a fellow disciple of mine, is not only a landscaping architect, but also a very learned Feng Shui expert and teacher, and she is one of the few people with expertise in both areas.

I admire this book for it pretty much covers all the information you need to know about how to DIY to incorporate Feng Shui into your garden design. The book starts off with the introduction of some theoretical background, such as the concept of Ch'i, Yin-Yang Philosophy and the Five Elements. Shelley goes on to explain the meaning and importance of Feng Shui. She also introduces Chinese landscaping in detail to readers, which contains a lot of Yin-Yang philosophy in terms of contrast and balance, solid and hidden, soft and strong, moving and still, etc. By working with the balance of Yin and Yang, it actually helps a person to go through the process of self-cultivation and personal growth in real life.

In addition to the detailed analysis of Feng Shui elements in garden design, Shelley also revealed many Feng Shui cures and adjustment methods to enhance all different aspects of our daily lives. The transcendental Feng Shui cures are one of the very unique features of Black Sect Tantric Buddhist Feng Shui theories. Shelley generously shares this precious knowledge with those who are fortunate enough to read this book and really follow the principles taught within.

I would like to congratulate Shelley for having done such a great job, and to congratulate all readers for having this complete guide of garden design with Feng Shui in your hand. It is truly my honor to write the foreword for this wonderful book.

September 13, 2011

Blessing

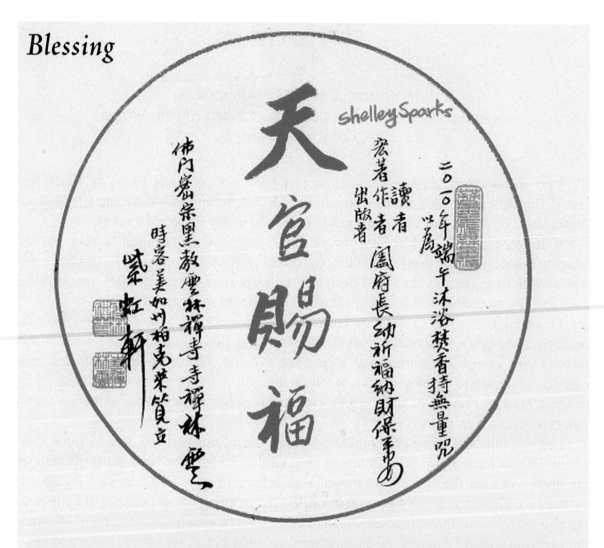

Translation: In the year of 2010 near Dragon Festival (which is Chinese lunar May 5th), after cleansing and incense offering, I chanted countless mantras to bestow blessings particularly upon Shelley Sparks' new book as well as herself, the publisher, and all readers, entire family including the elders, and the kids, for their safety and obtaining auspiciousness and wealth

Middle in red: The Heavenly Official bestowing all the fortune

Left: Lin Yun, Spiritual Leader of Black Sect Tantric Buddhism at Fourth Stage and the Abbot of Yun Lin Temple, wrote this calligraphy at Khadro Crystal Chu Rinpoche's study.

Introduction

When I began studying landscape architecture I wanted to be a steward and caretaker of the earth. I always felt the earth needed an advocate to preserve and protect it. Once I became a landscape architect my mission expanded to helping people create gardens that make them happy and get them involved with the earth. I realized that the very act of gardening and caring for plants is a meditative process. Working with plants produces an understanding of our connection to the earth and everything on it. As I worked my own garden and talked to other gardeners I learned that the garden could be a tremendous healing force in our life.

With this knowledge, my focus began to shift. Although I still wanted to create spaces that make people happy, I realized the potential to help people connect to their gardens and the earth in a more personal manner was more important. My role as a designer is to help people find a deeper meaning in their gardens so that there is more harmony and balance in their lives.

Throughout my life, I have been a skeptic. Anything that I can't see, touch, taste, hear, or smell will have to prove itself to me. My discovery of feng shui was serendipitous. I was offered a free class in something that purported to teach how to create a harmonious environment.

I was surprised when feng shui brought dramatic changes in my own life and I became a believer. Using feng shui in my home and garden brought me financial security, recognition, and a renewed sense of life purpose. The more I became involved with feng shui the deeper my spiritual life evolved.

Most people are attracted to feng shui because of the promise of more money, better relationships, and improved health. I have learned to appreciate the deep and meaningful philosophies behind feng shui. For example, I love knowing that the objects I use in feng shui connect to a long and reverent culture. Feng shui bonds me to an ancient ancestry, the earth, and my spiritual source.

Using feng shui principles to design a garden provides a framework for the plan of the garden. From the perspective of a landscape architect, feng shui offers good basic design principles with rich ideas about materials, colors, and shapes. From a gardener's perspective, feng shui provides a greater sense of delight because the garden elements become more meaningful. Feng shui captures the essence of nature in forms, shapes, and materials for the purpose of lifting the human spirit. What feng shui adds to garden design is intention and purpose so that the good feeling that gardeners experience working with plants can be extended to all parts of our lives.

Using feng shui in the garden not only helps to create a meaningful environment, but also helps bring about life changes that will make you happier. Some people wonder how meaningful it is to have more money, better relationships, and better health. It's difficult to think about spiritual matters when we are struggling with our health, finances, and relationships. The ultimate goal in using feng shui in our gardens is to heal ourselves. It is only through healing ourselves that we can best serve others and the earth.

Chapter 1

Seeing the Garden through New Eyes

Have you ever been in a garden that piqued your senses to the extent that you recall these sensations and the image of that space years later? If so, then you have experienced universal forces in harmony and balance. Whether you live in an apartment, the suburbs, or in the country, you can create and enjoy a wonderful garden by using feng shui principles

Feng shui is the ancient Chinese art of placement. When you arrange your environment using Feng shui, you can produce the life-changing results such as increased wealth, improved relationships, and enhanced health. As your environment comes into balance you can naturally manifest the best things in life. My favorite feng shui garden story comes from an esteemed colleague. She added an enhancement to the wealth area of her property. Her gardener copied it in his own garden and he won the lotto the following week!

Using feng shui in a garden promotes a new balance, harmony, and satisfaction because it enables us to arrange the garden in concert with earth's universal forces. Literally translated, *feng shui* means wind and water. The demands of the modern life push many of us away from the earth, causing a disconnection from this important element of life. This missing element can be fulfilled by having a garden.

The Magic of Feng Shui

To Westerners, feng shui is a magical and mysterious art. The Eastern concept of energy is a far cry from the logical mental construct that is familiar to most people. While you may not comprehend how adding a fragrant gardenia or a purple flowering plant will deeply affect you and balance your environment, know that it can. If you're skeptical, you're not alone. I felt the same way when I began studying feng shui. One of the first times I used feng shui principles, I was trying to find a tenant for a house that I owned. The house had been vacant for some time and I was starting to feel desperate. As soon as I placed flags in the garden areas of Wealth, Fame and Relationship, I quickly attracted a congenial tenant who willingly paid the high rent that I was seeking.

I now understand that the concept of energy that has been employed for centuries is merely a principle that the Western world has not *yet* been able to prove. Like the electron, a black hole, or the quark, the effects of energy can be seen or deduced. Millions of people can attest to the dramatic effects of shifting, adding, or moving energy through Chinese medicine, acupuncture and feng shui.

The Western work ethic has produced technological advances that have revolutionized society. Because of this, people believe that the harder they work, the more they will achieve. The Eastern concept of energy doesn't negate the work you do; it complements and enhances it. Using feng shui, you can produce the results you want without enormous sacrifices to your time and life. Energy and energy movement add an element that not only magnifies the results of your work but often brings advances in delightfully unexpected arenas. I worked with a lonely client who wanted more friendships in her life. After we enhanced the Relationship area of her yard, she not only found that she developed a more loyal group of friends, but an old boyfriend that she had given up on re-entered her life and they began to develop a whole new level of relationship.

Feng shui points the way to the areas in your life where you are out of balance. With feng shui, you may discover that your house may not support your highest potential or your garden may lack the energy to sustain life. Perhaps your house dominates the lot, leaving you with little outdoor space to enjoy. The lack or deficiency evident in your surroundings will express itself in your life. Conversely, as you use the principles of feng shui to build or change your home and garden, you will see improvement in your life.

A Garden's Delight

Who can resist a beautiful garden? The urge to create, visit, and bask in gardens is more than a passion for humans. Green space is your connection to nature. Your awareness of food, medicine, and clean air comes from working with nature. In our modern world contact with nature and your awareness of its regenerative powers may be severely limited. This is a missing link in your being that all primitive societies understand. People who are constantly surrounded by nature understand how to find and use medicinal plants and unique food sources. They understand the healing effects of nature.

Nature is a healing experience on many different levels. Many medicinal cures still come from plants– aspirin from the willow tree and heart medication from the beautiful foxglove, to mention two. Mere contact with nature can restore the human spirit. The more you engage your senses with nature and plants, the greater its effect on you. For instance, when you see a beautiful rock you can marvel at its shape and size, or you may be reminded of age and fortitude. If you touch its crags or lie on it, feeling warmth at the end of a sunny day, you can experience a greater level of joy relating to it. If you have beautiful plants in your environment, their effect will be magnified if you actually love and care for them. By caring for plants, you participate in the mystery of life; you contribute to growing and expanding the life force in the world.

Feng Shui and the Garden

Feng shui magnifies the healing effects of the garden. Through correct placement, plants and other elements can become powerful instruments of healing and benefice. Using plants that augment the healing process such as medicinal plants can add another element of power to feng shui solutions.

When I design gardens, I have so many great ideas- that sometimes it can be hard to decide which options to implement. By using feng shui principles as a road map, I found that it becomes easier to create a design based on what will produce the best results for my client's life.

If you use feng shui principles in your garden the shapes, concept, and elements you use in your design all have a purpose and a special significance for you.

No matter what a feng shui book may say, the most important thing to remember when designing your garden is to surround yourself with elements that you love and that make you happy. Because feng shui uses very specific options in the arrangement of items in the garden, you may add elements that you may not have otherwise considered. In other words, explore and reach for novel ideas, elements, and solutions. Planning your garden is half of the fun.

Every garden is a marriage between the house, the land, and the person who lives there. Because I encourage my clients to take an active role when I design their garden, the final

design turns out to be quite different from my original concept. It becomes their creation. Your garden will never be a generic "English garden" or "Japanese garden" because even if you design using perennial borders or oriental motifs you will have unique elements keyed to your own needs and desires.

Designing a garden using feng shui has all of the limitations of other methods of design. You won't be able to plant trees and shrubs that don't grow in your climate. You will have to work with the quality of soil typical to your lot. The challenges that face all garden designers when they develop concepts and execute them with style and beauty will also confront you in a feng shui garden. The key to using feng shui properly is to consistently be in tune with your heart's desire, your intuition, and the physical circumstances of your garden. A feng shui garden will provide you with rich possibilities, an expanded palette of choices, and a greater potential to manifest what you need and want in your life.

Intention of This book

This book is meant to be a guide. No one can give you cookie cutter advice on how to enhance your property, or instruct you in a "paint-by-numbers" fashion. That would not satisfy you, nor would it help you accomplish your life's goals. My intention is to provide you with some basic feng shui rules and information about the tools you can use to build, add, and change your garden to improve it and your life.

One of the most important tools used in feng shui assessment is a map known as the Ba-Gua. It offers many different opportunities for adding meaningful elements to improve your garden. The Ba-Gua can provide you with specific recommendations about the types of elements you may need to add throughout your property. For instance, placing a barbecue grill in one area may burn out your creativity; however, if you move it to a different location, it could attract the right kind of attention for your work. I offer many plant recommendations; however, don't just blindly select a listed plant. Plants are important living beings that you should relate to intimately. Find the plants you love for each location rather than blindly following anyone's recommendation. Do your own research. The Internet is an excellent resource for viewing pictures of plants that interest you and reading about their qualities.

The most important decisions you make for your garden should include elements that are meaningful to you. In this book, I have included some legends, meanings of plants, and other elements designed to captivate you and help you improve your life and your garden.

Using Your Intuition

Through many years of meditation and communing with the land, I acquired the ability to sense and listen to the earth. For some people, intuition comes more naturally. Every property is a mix of the land itself, the building architecture, and the people who live or work there. Sometimes, either singularly or together, something in the mix cries out for a different idea. The garden and the house offer information that might not otherwise have been known. For instance, some locations always seem to have failed enterprises such as divorces or bankruptcies. This information can be determined just by looking at the house, lot, or land configuration or slope. Knowing this can help the current residents make the additions or changes necessary to avoid the same fate as their predecessors. A unique solution to the landscape design is born from the need of the land, building or people. I will show you specific examples of how to design a property, and explain the thought processes involved in adapting uncommon solutions to challenging prospects.

Beyond the Garden

What lies beyond the garden gate? Why do people spend hundreds of hours toiling for a garden that is wiped out by snow in the winter? What is beyond the wealth, health, relationships and fame that people seek through feng shui? When you begin working with feng shui principles, you may only want to get out of a financial jam or find your true soul mate. Feng shui has become popular because it can help you turn your life around. This is enough for many people, but feng shui can offer you more. You have the potential to grow spiritually through practicing feng shui. Spiritual growth is not a religious or an unfathomable aim. It is attained by trusting the flow of life. Understanding the seasons and constant shifting of life will help you live with tranquility in your heart. This is the same enlightenment that gardeners achieve through building a garden. Imagine how your garden can provide a context for spiritual enlightenment.

Feng shui and gardening can work hand in hand to propel you along your life path. Gardening gives you physical proof of manifestation. No matter how low maintenance your garden may be, you will always be aware of the cycles and the capriciousness of life. If you already work in a garden, you understand how captivating and miraculous it is to nurture living things and watch them grow.

Feng shui can help you by adding significance to your garden. Along with the elements, shapes, and intentions that feng shui adds, you can also include ceremonies that augment your relationship to your property.

For thousands of years, ceremonies have been people's primary connection to their spiritual side. Most civilizations conducted their ceremonies in sacred spaces on their land. Their land became special through the ceremonies they conducted. In feng shui terms, you are increasing the energy of the earth by consecrating your part of it.

Many Roads, the Same Path

People learn about themselves and life through many different ways. Sports, art, automobiles, animals, computers, gardening, religion, and metaphysics all provide ways to learn about yourself and your place in the world. In each arena there are different paths that you can choose. For instance, I have developed my awareness through feng shui, gardening, sports, meditation, metaphysics, and animals. I love hiking, running, and swimming. You may love to play golf or tennis. All of the choices you make in your life come together to make the unique package that is yours so you can lend your energy to help make the world better.

There are many different schools in the world of feng shui. Each school offers its own form of wisdom. I chose the Black Sect Tantric School of feng shui, founded by His Holiness Grandmaster Lin Yun Rinpoche. This school incorporates Buddhism, Confucianism, Taoism, Yin-Yang philosophy, I-Ching, and Chinese folklore as well as the modern sciences of geology, hydrology, psychology, philosophy, and others. What attracted me to this method is His Holiness's emphasis on modern applications to ancient traditions and the spirituality. I have learned from his compassion, wisdom, and strength. In bringing this knowledge to the West, he incorporated many forms of Western knowledge and expanded his teachings for the benefit of all.

As you use this book, remember to bring your own special gifts to your garden. You stand here as the result of every teacher, relative, and friend that you have known. There are no right or wrong decisions, only new paths of learning and self-growth.

Chapter 2

Starting at Bedrock

When I began gardening, my ambition was limited to putting pretty plants into the ground. I was only moderately successful because I lacked the knowledge of soil fertility and the proper conditions for specific types of plants. Likewise, learning the basics of feng shui takes patience. At first, it might seem difficult to understand how to apply it to your property or garden. Some people tell me there are too many things to think about. In this chapter we will start to accumulate the basics. You don't have to know everything all at once. Trust that the right solution will come to you at the right time. Just remember this: the foundation you build with feng shui knowledge will bring you greater understanding of feng shui, the garden and yourself.

About Feng Shui

Though the principles of feng shui were formulated in China, its origins are much older and universal. Feng shui principles teach people to provide a safe, secure, and harmonious space in which to live. Knowledge of the earth and secure environments is instinctive for indigenous people who depend on this information to live. Grandmaster Lin said, "Feng shui began the first time man crawled into the cave or built a tree house because in that place and time, they were selecting the safest environment for themselves." Feng shui endures and thrives in the twenty-first century because it is adaptable. It responds to our instinct to correct our environment so we feel comfortable and our lives run more smoothly.

Feng shui originated approximately 3,000-4,000 years ago in China. It began as a method for siting graves, as it was thought that if your ancestors were well placed they would assist your life. It was adapted to houses because people observed how particular placements affected the fortunes and misfortunes of their neighbors. They observed that good fortune results when one's house and land are placed in a way that is harmonious with the forces of nature. Conversely, disasters can occur when a house is not well placed. We only need to watch the news for confirmation. In California, where houses are overbuilt on unstable hills, mudslides and earthquakes correct this condition. When we build in flood plains, we see people are displaced by floods. These principles extend to less dramatic situations in everyday life. Multinational hotel corporations use feng shui to ensure profitable units, and small apartment dwellers use the principles to add harmony to their daily living.

Much of the basis for feng shui is drawn from *I Ching,* also known as the *Book of Changes.* The *I Ching* dates back about 4,000 years and is a book originally used for divination. The system is built on trigrams, three lines that are either broken or unbroken. The unbroken lines represent yang energy and the broken lines represent yin energy. There are eight different combinations and each arrangement of lines has several layers of meanings. For instance, three unbroken lines represent the concept of heaven and in terms of the family, it is the father and in the body it is the head.

When two trigrams are combined they create a hexagram that is used in the divination. Over time the *I Ching* has come to have a wider use. It is a book of wisdom which describes the laws of nature i.e. how opposite forces are used to define each other, how equilibrium always asserts itself and how change is inevitable. It helps people understand how to attain a balanced way of life. Chinese medicine, acupuncture and feng shui, among other practices use information of the *I Ching* to help people align themselves with a healthy equilibrium. One of our most important tools, the Ba-Gua uses the *I Ching* trigrams which represent different aspects of life.

Like many of the world's disciplines, feng shui has changed and grown as it has moved throughout China and to the rest of the world. Since I have been teaching feng shui, I discovered

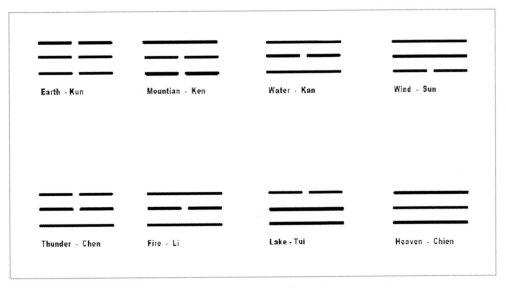

Ill 2-1 Each of the *I Ching* trigrams has a different meaning

that many don't understand that there are many different schools of feng shui, each of which has a different orientation.

One early school of feng shui developed in rural China is known as the *Form School*. It uses the forms and directions of mountains, hills valleys and water masses to assess the best location for a home and its elements. This school references the White Tiger, Green Dragon, Black Tortoise, Red Phoenix and Golden Snake.

The different schools of *Classical Feng Shui* employ a compass to relate the directions, the stars and a person's Chinese birthday in order to determine the healthiest and most auspicious placement of a home and objects. When you read about north, south, east, and west, and see a chart with birth dates and directions, you are reading about the Compass School.

The Black Sect Tantric Buddhist School popularized feng shui in America. This sect founded by His Holiness Grandmaster Lin Yun Rinpoche and now led by Her Holiness Khadro Crystal Chu Rinpoche made feng shui accessible to the average person. This school uses the Ba-Gua as a tool to assess a property.

As feng shui has become more widely known and used, other schools have proliferated. Some of them emphasize one aspect of the practice or another. Many of them have valuable information to convey. I always tell my students to be aware of the different schools because confusing the information from one school with another as I did in my early days of studies can be frustrating and lead to inaccurate diagnoses.

Ch'i-The Life Force

In order to design a garden where the energy flows properly, one first must understand what energy is. Energy, or *ch'i,* is the life force underlying everything. This force animates everything -people, animals, plants, rocks, and the earth itself. Everything is infused with ch'i. It is a very fluid force, that moves through all things.

Quantum physics teaches us that all material things are made up of atoms. An atom is not a solid entity. It is an expression of energy and movement in constant motion and change. Even our thought processes are energy and movement. The difference between atoms inside our bodies and atoms in a rock or a tree is their arrangement and quantity. Our bodies are just a bit denser than what is "thin air." Atoms move freely from our bodies to mingle in our surroundings and vice versa. Our knowledge of quantum physics has set the stage for the link to the Chinese concept of ch'i.

Describing ch'i in this limited form actually diminishes its true role. More significantly, ch'i is a universal force. It is what we might call the force that creates and drives the laws of nature. When we view ch'i in terms of a spiritual force, we may think in Western terms of heaven or God. When we view ch'i in terms of an earthly force, we think of the laws of nature. The third kind of ch'i is found in humans individually and as a society. Each of these types of ch'i is interconnected.

Feng shui helps people select, create, or build the healthiest environments for them. By evaluating the ch'i of your land, neighborhood, house, and garden you can find or arrange the environment in such a way as to attract good and free-flowing energy. If you doubt your ability to sense ch'i in a garden, think back to a time when plants were overcrowded and overgrown in your yard. Can you remember what a difference it made when they were trimmed properly or removed? Another common garden experience happens when you see a lawn turn brown in the fall or winter and then observe the miracle of new blades of grass in the spring. You may have seen gardens that look like pages from *Garden Beautiful* but they may have left you with no feeling, and conversely a seemingly plain garden space may have some special charm that brings you a sense of familiarity that just feels right. The dramatic changes that occur in short periods of time can help us understand how a shift in the energy in our yards can make a big effect on how we feel. The long-term lack of ch'i in our environment does have a serious effect on our lives and our fortunes.

Much of what we learn through Western science methods has been used for centuries in folk cultures. For instance when I started studying feng shui I was surprised to learn many of the principles are used by civil engineers, architects and landscape designers when they design roads, homes and gardens.

Yin and Yang - Balance in the Life Force

The natural or optimal state of ch'i is always to be in both balance and change. The ideas of balance and change are expressed in the concepts of *yin* and *yang*. The most perfect form of these two energies is illustrated by the Tai Chi, which shows the white *yang energy* flowing into and complementing the black *yin energy*. Each part has a spot on the other to temper and complete it.

Yang energy is outgoing, bright, active, upward, aggressive, and masculine. Yin energy is receptive, dark, passive, downward, intuitive, and feminine. Harmony occurs when they are in balance. These forces are a part of us and affect our lives. Yang energizes us, gets us going, is bright, and helps us make things happen in our lives. This is its healthy effect on us. If we possess too much of this aspect, our growth as a human being may be stunted because we may not examine ourselves and our motives. An excess of yang energy may make us too aggressive or cause us to wear ourselves out because we are overactive.

Ill. 2-2 The Tai Ch'i symbol represents the perfect balance between yin and yang.

Yin energy is our receptive, intuitive, passive, and knowing side. Yin energy helps us examine and evaluate where we are on life's path and where we are going. This is our nurturing side, the side that is giving and empathetic to others. When we have too much yin we may become self-centered, depressed, reclusive and feel drained. We may find ourselves giving too much to others without taking our own needs into account. Both yang and yin need the balance of the other to be in harmony.

The earth shows us how yin and yang come together in balance on a physical level. On land, rocks and water often naturally occur together. Water flows from the mountains and collects in lakes below, and mountains are often lifted from the edge of oceans. Yin and yang work together in balance where water flows over rocks and where rocks rise out of the water. Some view mountains as yang because of their upward shape and water as yin because it yields to all shapes, which is a receptive quality. These positions can be reversed when viewed in terms of active and passive, where water is an active yang force and the mountain at rest is yin passive energy. Rocks alone can be an expression of these two eternal forces--their shapes show the upward thrusts of geological forces and alternatively the crevices and depressions show the wear of time. Water, too, can exhibit both yin and yang properties. A still lake is passive, quiet yin force while a bubbling stream or river is active yang. This is what is meant by yang being expressed in yin and yin being expressed in yang.

Rocks and water are not the most common example of yin and yang in our gardens. The play between shadows and light is an important aspect that needs to be balanced. A garden that is too dark contains too much yin and can be a dull, depressing space that does not conduct good ch'i. Conversely, a southern or western exposure garden with no shade or cooling effects contains too much yang and is too hot and uncomfortable for energy to flow properly.

Yin-yang balance also works in choosing colors for the garden. If you use primarily reds, oranges, and yellows in your garden, the yang nature of these colors can tire you out like the southern exposure. If you choose only blue or dark purple, it can make the garden too drab and somber. When using colors we seek a balance of energies; so if you love, love, love yellow flowers, balance them out with purple flowers. If you don't like any of the cool colors, you can always use white to help soften the extremes of too much cool energy or too much hot energy. With white, make sure that the proportion of white flowers does not dominate the composition because in the Chinese vernacular, white represents death. Therefore, use white sparingly.

The Five Elements

The five elements, water, wood, fire, earth, and metal, are earthly manifestations of the interplay of yin and yang. These elements are the way ch'i interacts within and between people and the natural environment. *I Ching* teaches us that these elements may seem tangible, but they are really forces rather than materials. The forces they exert are as follows:

- <u>Water</u> is a fluid, gathering, or dispersing movement.

- <u>Wood</u> is upward, expansive, and creative movement.

- <u>Fire</u> is an expansive, explosive, hot movement.

- <u>Earth</u> is a stable, firm, reliable movement.

- <u>Metal</u> is a contracting, cold, heavy, inward movement.

Each element has a shape, color, season, and several physical manifestations. They are used as an additional method of analyzing, balancing and harmonizing the ch'i of the land, people, and gardens. The five elements have relationships to each other that teach us how to bring balance to an aspect that is out of equilibrium.

The Ba-Gua — a Universal Map of Harmony

The Ba-Gua is the map which puts many of the ideas of feng shui and balance into practice on your property. Using the Ba-Gua, we can diagnose your property to find its balances and imbalances. It employs ch'i, yin and yang, the five elements, and many deeper ideas. With these tools we can create environments that support prosperity, good relationships, and good health.

The Ba-Gua is separated into eight sections. Each section or Gua has a color, symbol, and physical aspect drawn from *I Ching*, parts of the body, a life situation and other aspects. Four of the Guas and the center have one of the five elements associated with it. Of course, the most interesting aspect of each of the Guas is the life situations they represent and how it relates to us.

The Ba-Gua outlines the specific areas of life that can be addressed by working with feng shui. Let's identify the areas of life which we can work toward building a better future.

I like to start with Ch'ien, which is the Benefactors or Helpful People area of the Ba-Gua. This area also governs travel. The symbol- Ch'ien- translates from *I Ching* as "heaven." This meaning shows the quality of help that comes our way when this area has good ch'i. This area brings help whether or not we have asked for it. Help appears in our lives as if "from heaven." The kinds of issues that can show up in this area are whether or not people help you or people stand in your way and oppose your efforts. As this area also governs travel, issues of safety in travel and frequency of travel may come into play.

The next area is the K'an or Career area of the Ba-Gua, represented by the element of water. This area indicates the flow and the foundation of life and represents what we give to the world in terms of our work or our life mission. It is not only connected to our career but also to our wealth. Like water, this area can be deep and still or influenced by other forces and turbulent. Issues that show up in this area are missed opportunities to do our life's work, problems in our work environment, roadblocks in our career, or not being able to translate our work into a means of financial support.

The Ken or Knowledge area of the Ba-Gua governs book knowledge, spiritual knowledge, and most importantly self-knowledge or contemplation. The *I Ching* symbol Ken- translates as "mountain." The mountain is still within and allows for time and processes to wear on it. Like the mountain, we can acquire knowledge, spirituality, and self-growth by being still and reflecting on the lessons the world is offering us. Issues in this area show up as trouble learning, continually making the same mistakes, or difficulty connecting with our spiritual side.

The Chen or Family area of the Ba-Gua is the area of our ancestors, family lineage, or connection with people older than us. The *I Ching* symbol for this area is "thunder" and is represented by the element of wood. It is here we find our support or foundation. I always think of the quote from the movie "*Amistad*", "I stand here as the reason my ancestors lived". Indeed we do carry the burden or the gift of being our ancestors' representative in our genes. Besides our traditional ancestors, this area also represents our mentors or teachers, and other family-like support systems. Issues in this area may be expressed as problems with our parents, childhood problems, an inability to get along with elders, or lack of support systems and foundations.

Because it represents Wealth, the Sun area is a favorite area for many of my clients and students. The *I Ching* symbol here is "wind." Wind is an energy that acts in invisible ways to achieve visible results. It is the energy for material and non-material wealth--for good luck and money. Issues in this area are money problems, not only not making money but also the inability to keep money.

The next area, <u>Li</u> is known as the <u>Fame</u> area of the Ba-Gua and is represented by the element of fire. The I Ching symbol is also "fire." This area governs ambition and reputation, the effect of your work in the world, your ability to get promoted or promote yourself, and your standing in the community. It also represents illumination and clarity. Issues in this area can result in one becoming infamous rather than famous. A poor reputation or lack of recognition in your field of work or business can be the result of poor feng shui in Li.

The next area of the Ba-Gua, <u>K'un</u> or <u>Marriage,</u> (also marriage like relationships) is another popular area. The *I Ching* symbol for this area is "earth." This area governs marriage, close loving relationships, and partnerships. Problems in this area include marriage issues and problems finding the right partners and friends.

The last area of the Ba-Gua area is <u>Tui</u> or <u>Children</u>, represented by the element of metal. The *I Ching* symbol translated means "lake." This area governs all of your children, your descendants, and everyone younger than you. Issues in this area manifest as fertility problems or problems with children and other young people.

The center of the Ba-Gua is not considered Gua or section. It is the "catch all" for the other eight sections. It carries the element of earth and it governs any issues not addressed specifically in the Guas, especially health. In my experience, when things aren't working well in some of the Gua areas, it has an impact on the center. It is easy to see how when we have major problems in one aspect of our lives, it can impact our health. The issues here manifest as physical, emotional, or spiritual health problems.

The Ba-Gua is actually a map with meaning. When we apply this map to a person's land, garden, home, or business space, we can help them resolve the issues of their lives, to help them produce positive changes.

Applying the Ba-Gua to Land

The Ba-Gua is applied to a piece of land and a house from an aerial point of view. Gardeners are familiar with drawing plans to designate where plants are to be installed. This is the same process for the entire property and for the house. The best place to begin is with a survey or plot plan of your property with the house shown in place. You can also get a strong sense of this if you look at the Google Earth view of your property. Sometimes when you buy a house the appraiser will produce a plan of the property and house for you.

BA-GUA

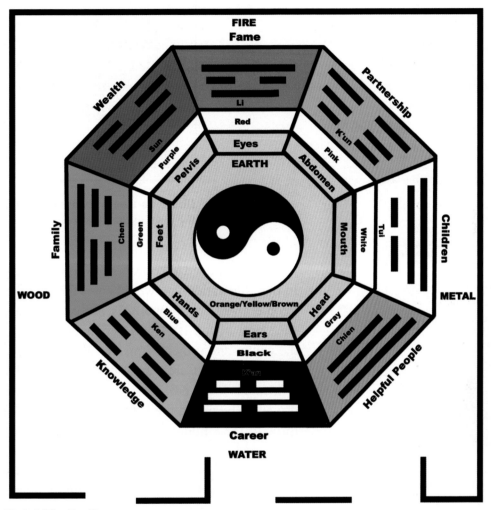

Ill. 2-3 The Ba-Gua

The easiest way to apply the Ba-Gua to a piece of land is to first divide the property into nine equal parts. Although the Ba-Gua shown in this illustration is an octagon, for practical purposes it can be applied to any property as a square or rectangle. Next, find the largest or major entry, which would usually be the driveway or front walkway. Then place Knowledge, Career, and Helpful People areas along the entry line. The rest of the Guas follow in order of the Ba-Gua. Another way to say this is you will always enter your property either through the Knowledge, Career or Helpful People area.

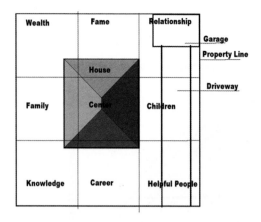

Ill. 2-4 Applying the Ba-Gua

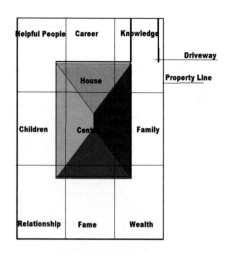

Ill. 2-5 Ba-Gua is always applied from the front of the property

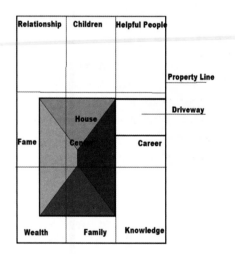

Ill. 2-6 The Ba- Gua oriented from a different direction

Next we need to know how to apply it to a property. In this illustration you would enter through the Helpful People area. This property is perfectly square so that each part of the Ba-Gua is complete. The house fills the center and projects into the Wealth, Fame, Family, Knowledge and Career areas of the Ba-Gua. The garage is located in the partnership or Marriage area and the driveway begins in the Helpful People area and moves through the Children's area and into the Relationship area.

A square or a rectangle shaped lot or house allows for the Ba-Gua to be "complete" without missing areas. In a rectangular property it is stretched into nine equal rectangular shapes. Illustrations 2-5 and 2-6 show the entry to a property in the Career and Knowledge areas, respectively, on rectangular properties. I have oriented the door on different sides of the illustrations to demonstrate that no matter where the entry is, north, south, east, west, the application of the Ba-Gua is always oriented to the entry of the property.

The Ba-Gua is a complete shape but many of our houses and lots are not perfect squares or rectangles. Illustration 2-7 shows a flag lot that enters from the Helpful People area. The Knowledge area and parts of the Career, Family and Center areas are missing. This will result in missing potential in all of these arenas of life. How do you determine when you have a missing area? First you must look at the overall plan to see if it is perfectly square or rectangular. If it

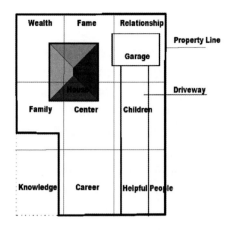

Ill. 2-7 A flag lot has missing areas.

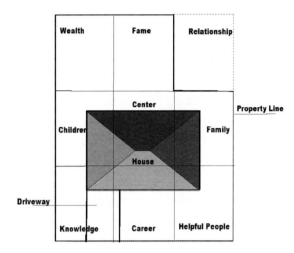

Ill. 2-9 Extension in Relationship area.

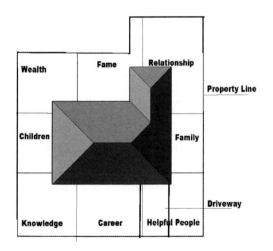

Ill. 2-8 Missing area in Relationship

is not, draw a line so that it becomes perfectly rectangular or square, and then examine the cut-out area. Where there is a cut out with less than 1/2 the length or width of the property, the area is considered to be a missing part, or missing potential.

Here we see another example of a missing area. Illustration 2-8 shows missing potential in the Relationship area, so we can expect that issues in partnerships may arise for the people living in this house.

Where the area beyond the perfect square or rectangle is less than one-half the length of the property, the area is considered an extension, as in the illustration 2-9. Here we see the entry is in the Helpful People area, and there is an extension in the Relationship area. Additionally, there is an extension to the house. Where there are extensions, generally speaking, there is added potential or bonus energy.

Cures and Enhancements, aka Method of Minor Additions

What do you do when you have a property or a house that has a missing piece? In the last section we learned that missing pieces represent missing the potential for certain arenas in our life. The good news is that feng shui offers solutions to help fill in missing areas as well as fix conditions where ch'i is not flowing properly in a house or property.

There are many reasons why energy may not flow well on a piece of property. Besides the shape of the property or shape of the house, the land may have innate problems. The neighborhood, neighboring people, or other elements may be affecting your land. The slope of the land may not be conducive to good energy flow. The relationship between the land and the street could also be problematic. All of these conditions and many more situations can be addressed using feng shui cures. These cures can also help people whose houses have complete shapes but who have problematic life situations. Situations where land, neighbors and other external factors need to be addressed will be explored in later chapters.

Cures or enhancements are physical elements that are arranged, moved, added, or removed to shift the ch'i or energy of a condition. These cures or enhancements can make dramatic changes in a person's fortune. Cures are designed to bring the environment back to health and remedy the problems in our lives caused by the imbalances in our surroundings. By adding minor objects or making minor changes, you can realize huge results.

Cures and enhancements work to change the focus and energy flow of the environment. Some of the objects used do not make "sense" in terms of our Western thinking, but have been used for centuries to change the balance of energy in a space. A major factor in shifting energy in a space is using the cures along with our intention to bring about change. Making changes in our lives is often difficult. With feng shui, you will find that placing objects and identifying a shift in intention can produce the major changes you seek.

Making feng shui changes can work wonders but I want to emphasize that it doesn't work alone. You must put in the effort necessary to accomplish the task. For instance, if you place a feng shui cure with the intention of selling a house and then you don't market the house or price it competitively, your chances of success are better but are still not good. You have to do what needs to be done in the worldly sense to get the results you seek. Feng shui alone usually doesn't do it. Bearing that in mind, feng shui is an amazing practice to help all the elements of luck line up in your corner.

Cures and Enhancements— A sample list of objects

1. <u>Light producing or refracting objects</u>: Mirrors, crystals, lighting

2. <u>Sound producing elements</u>: Wind chimes, music, birds and bees in the garden

3. <u>Life force elements</u>: Fish, pets, wild animals, bonsai, plants, landscaping

4. <u>Weight and heavy objects</u>: Statues, rocks, walls, sculptures

5. <u>Color</u>: Colors of the five elements, Ba-Gua, Rainbow Colors, Six True Colors

6. <u>Moving objects</u>: Windmills, whirligigs, flags, mobiles, wind vanes, fans

7. <u>Water elements</u>: Water sculptures, fountains, bird baths

8. <u>Energy or fire producing objects</u>: Barbecues, fire pits, candles, firecrackers

9. <u>Others</u>: Constructed additions such as gazebos, overhead structures, bridges; sacred shapes or motifs used in various ways; specialty cures; bamboo; fragrances; transcendental methods or objects

Different cures are used for specific situations. Sometimes the same object will be used in different ways with different objectives in mind. For instance, water fountains may be used to create a harmonious setting at a house entry, or they may be used to attract and circulate money to the home. There are certain situations where we know we will always need cures. Cures will be needed wherever your situation is unhappy, unfortunate or needs change. I will provide more specific information about cures in future chapters.

I will describe many elements for the garden and feng shui. Some of them will appeal to your sensibilities and others won't engage you at all. If a particular element sounds or feels right, it is something that you should consider including in your garden. If an element doesn't seem to work for you, perhaps you should not consider using it in your garden. I have worked with people who do not like certain types of feng shui solutions, either for

Wind Chimes should have high clear sounds

the aesthetics or for the lack of connection to the object. Although incorporating some of the traditional elements brings forth all of the meaning inherent from that element, it is paramount what you include in your garden are objects, plants, and designs that you love. Being the creator, you must love what you create.

Using Feng Shui to Organize a Garden

Designing a garden is a complex and individual act. Garden spaces can be a haven, a healing space, a place for play, a place for meditation, or all of these things and more. You will have your own ideas of how your perfect garden will take shape and what feeling you want to create. What you seek to accomplish in your garden can be incorporated into any garden design.

Designing a garden using feng shui principles provides you with a structure and tools to help you organize the flow and the elements in the garden. There are principles of feng shui which can help garden organization and ideals of garden design that align with feng shui principles. Our aim is to create spaces that are balanced and harmonious. How we design the entry walk, what we include to balance the design elements, and which shapes are expressed in a garden all help to create the composition that will enhance the positive flow of your life.

The concepts of ch'i, yin and yang, and the Ba-Gua have been introduced to provide a basis for the principles that will be employed in the garden. We will use the Ba-Gua map to explore the lacks or uncertainties that problematic landforms or shapes may create in our lives or to augment the areas that we want to improve. By introducing cures we will provide ways to enhance the garden. Balancing the yin and yang and the five elements will be an important part of creating your garden, as well as introducing any of the elements or concepts of Chinese garden design that may be appropriate.

For instance, if you are looking for a new career and your entry walkway is in the Career area of the Ba-Gua, you would want to be sure the walk is in good repair, well lit, and not blocked by plants. Another approach to this area would be to use a representation of the Career area from the Ba-Gua, water, to enhance this area. Creating a garden this way, we use the metaphors of not blocking a path, lighting a path, being sure that there is stability, and adding the flow of water to help you to manifest the opportunities of life.

The Benefits of a Feng Shui Garden

When a landscape is designed as an experiential joy and the spaces seem to "flow" well, then the concepts that are employed are very compatible between feng shui and good garden design. This kind of garden is bound to be a life-enhancing space. When a garden is beautiful and sensual to us or when it provides us with positive emotional experiences, the energy is often flowing correctly.

Good garden design requires that your needs are met for the use of the property, your aesthetic desires are addressed, you are sensitive to the land and the environment, and you marry the design of the landscape to the design of the home. The best feng shui principles require that you are sensitive to the environment - you design in order to create good energy flow of the land, use natural elements to create aesthetically pleasing compositions, and create spaces that have meaning beyond the garden's physical beauty. Matching good garden design with good feng shui principles is highly compatible and serves to enrich both the garden and us. We are actually getting two for one - all of the enjoyment of a wonderful garden design and a garden that will improve our lives!

When a space is created with intention and knowledge of energy flows, we can bring into view the best possibilities for our future. Designing a garden that expresses your hopes, dreams, and desires helps to call forth these ideals for your future. Defining your hopes, dreams, or ideals clearly establishes your intention. This intention can then be expressed in the design of your garden. For example, if you intend to create more abundance or wealth in your life or to free yourself from financial burdens, enhancing the Wealth area of the garden will help to produce it.

Gardens with Meaning

Begin with the reasons you want to create a garden space - what is your intention in designing it? Our Western culture has much to learn about setting an intention for gardens. In Chinese and Japanese gardens, there is a purpose and meaning behind the design that somehow touches us deeply. In these gardens, the intention is to recreate nature for the purpose of lifting the human spirit. We see and feel a beauty and a sense of peace that alters our mood and lifts our spirit. Perhaps this is what we find so fascinating about them. In designing a new garden or remodeling a garden, we can learn to capture this aspect for our own spaces.

One of the basic tenets of feng shui is that your environment mirrors and shapes you. This means that everything that is used in the garden is important. The physical manifestation of our spaces reveals much about us. I have been in homes and gardens where clients have become so used to seeing their surroundings that they were unable to look at them objectively. If the interior of your home is disorganized and jumbled you may be stuck and have trouble moving forward in life. You may have blocks to your future achievements. In the garden, when you have a dead tree or a jumble of weeds in your Knowledge area, you may have trouble using your wisdom to guide you to a better life.

Understanding the Purpose for Your Garden

What is the nature of the space you are working with? If you have a small space and are trying to have a playground for your children and a space for meditation, this may not be possible, at least not at the same time.

Objectives List

* ***What Do You Want to Achieve?***

_____Active space for play or entertainment

_____Passive space for quiet meditation

_____Both

* ***What Life Goals Do You Want to Attain?***

_____More spirituality

_____More prosperity

_____Better health

_____Better relationships

_____More supportive family relations

_____More creativity

_____Better career

_____More acknowledgment or better reputation

_____Attracting helpful people

_____More knowledge or wisdom

_____All of the above

What you want to achieve in a garden space is a typical organizational question that a landscape architect or designer asks. If the intention is to create an active space, we need to know what kind of activities will be enjoyed in the space and how much room would be needed for each activity. If the intention is to create a meditative space, we need to know how private the space needs to be and what forms of meditation will be done here. For instance, walking meditation is becoming revitalized. Sometimes sacred shapes such as labyrinths are created on the land to encourage this activity. If your garden space is to be designed for both active and quiet spaces, all of the above considerations must be addressed and thought must be given to the graceful separation of the two functions.

When you examine the areas of the Ba-Gua and the objectives listed, you can see that they match. Finding an objective and then enhancing the area of your property that relates to that objective will provide results in your life.

Appealing to the Senses

Seeing, hearing, tasting, smelling, and touching plants have a profound effect on the way we feel when we are in the garden. <u>Vision</u> is the first sense that most of us think of when we think of the garden. The soothing greens or the beautiful colors of various plants can be unforgettable. Color has a dramatic and profound effect on us, especially when we view it every day. Color preferences are personal and very important to the way you feel about the garden and the way you feel in the garden. If you aren't sure of your color preferences, some clues may lie in the colors you use in your home or clothing.

<u>Smell</u> is our most basic instinctual sense. For centuries aromatherapy has been used as a healing element for people who are ailing physically or emotionally. Finding the plants that heal your particular physical or emotional weakness and using them in your garden can be a source of benefit to you. Some common herbs are known to help your emotional state. For instance, lavender is refreshing, relaxing, analgesic, and antiseptic. Smell preferences in the garden are highly personal too.

Our sense of <u>Taste</u> allows us to savor the flavors of herbs that may have healing qualities. Herbs are still the primary source of medical care for most of the world. Many of these plants can be grown in your garden. For instance, Chamomile, which induces sleep, is good for head colds, headaches, and stomachaches. In addition to the physical healing properties of these plants, Edward Bach, an English physician, developed a system of remedies based on plants that are thought to identify cures for people's psychological problems. For example, Willow trees support the restoration of a system depleted by bitterness and resentment. You can use other systems that have been developed by other healers or societies.

<u>Touch</u> is another way we can use our senses in the garden to heal. The different textures of plants can delight and comfort us, not only by touching them but also by seeing their various textures. Think about touching lamb's ears, a furry gray plant, or a succulent plant like ice plants or moss. Other ways that plants touch you is through their healing uses in massage. Massage reconnects you through touch to other humans and has been proven to improve self-esteem. Oils such as almond, apricot, and wheat germ assist in softening the skin and adding vitamins.

Our sense of <u>Hearing</u> allows us to enjoy the soothing sounds of water falling, the sounds of birds, the buzzing of bees and wind rustling through the grass, leaves, or bamboo. These sounds can delight and calm us. You can encourage this by using plants that attract birds, bees, or insects or using plants that make sounds in the wind such as grasses and bamboos, eucalyptus and palms.

There is a strong link between healing gardens and feng shui. Review the cures and note that sound producing, color (visual), moving (tactile), and fragrance are among the recommended enhancements. For centuries, Chinese gardens have used plants for all of their healing effects, including herbs that are found in Chinese medicine. Sense memories from childhood can't be ignored and often have a strong influence on what become our favorite plants in the garden.

There is good reason to be fascinated with Chinese gardens. We see many of the feng shui ideals in play when we look at these gardens. For a landscape architect it is equally important to see good basic design principles. I don't expect you to become a garden designer by reading this book, but you can use the next chapter as a tool to understand what designers use to create gardens that will be inexplicably satisfying.

Chapter 3

Adding the Soil

Designing a garden can be either an artistic talent or a learned response. When I began studying landscape architecture, I didn't know the name of any plant or even how to draw stick figures. My teachers and mentors taught me ideas and principles but until I started to see them work I wasn't able to use them properly. If you plan to design your own garden, I suggest that you read this chapter first, and then visit some gardens to see if you have feelings in each space. After each visit, quiz yourself to see what is "right" or "wrong" with each garden. Remember, your feelings come first. This should give you an opportunity to use your intuition first and then your intellect to analyze what feeds or depletes a space. If you don't get feelings at first, don't worry, they will develop with time.

History of Chinese Garden Design

From the old Yuyuan Garden in Shanghai to the many gardens in Suzhou you can see the principles of feng shui at work. In this chapter we will review aspects of Chinese gardens to offer you more options to incorporate in your garden. Use whatever appeals to you, materially or theologically.

Few books were written during thousands of years of Chinese garden design but visual evidence of gardens is represented in landscape paintings and poetry. Descriptive poetry and books about how to paint landscapes were written but little was said about designing a landscape space. Writing about landscape painting, an ancient Chinese poet, Hsien Ho, advised us to capture the "circulating breath" that animates scenes. He also instructed us to enter a garden scene and find just the right rocks, water, and plants that would uncover the hidden language that all these objects embody in nature.

Yuen Yeh, one book written instructing people about designing gardens, did not state rules. The individual was advised to call forth from their feelings a unique expression of creating a garden - the gardener's intuition.

> "The things that you love captivate you. They appear to your eyes and
> affect your heart. Your thoughts will fly more quickly than the brush.
> The path will wend this way and that; one's normal perspectives change
> and adapt themselves to the transformations from bright to shadowy,
> open to closed, dry to waterside. A thousand images flood in, prompted
> by the numerous allusions to the great tradition inscribed along the
> spectator's route and the garden has become the nursery of images and
> the hatching of a poetic trance. The flowers gleam in red and violet.
> There are magical beings everywhere. You can drink your wine like
> an old philosopher or an official who has done with his career and in
> your leisure, write poetry. Inspiration will be stirred by the fresh plants."
> Chi Ch'eng

Religious Movements through China

Gardens were originally found, not made. There always have been spaces considered special because of the way they are perceived.

In China, as in most traditions, outdoor spaces that later became temples and key buildings may have once been the grounds for magical ceremonies. Shamans used special outdoor spaces to heal people in need. These areas were a stage for ritual encounters between people and the universe-a magical association that many Chinese gardens have retained.

Each era and religious movement that moved through China affected garden design. The garden was not just used for pleasure; it was also used for intellectual, spiritual, and moral pursuits. Confucianism brought forth the idea that the garden is a place to find recreation in the arts and a place of self-cultivation. Careful husbandry or caring for the garden and the land became important under Confucius. Self-cultivation through fellowship was an important ideal. Gardens became an important place to gather and the structures offered further enrichment to their relationship to the garden. Thus we see the development of the Ting or garden pavilion, a structure which precedes the gazebo or pergola. The house which opened to the garden was designed to maximize the opportunity to entertain family and friends and for use in study and contemplation. Confucius used aspects of nature to describe or symbolize man's virtues. For example, bamboo, because it grows in clumps means friendship and support.

Taoism's profound identification with the right path comes with intense study of the natural world - harmonizing one's rhythm to the seasons and learning from nature. Nature is an equal in life's plans and man is only one part of the scheme. Natural asymmetrical shapes are used in the garden because perfect symmetry is rarely seen in nature. Yin-Yang symbolism is emphasized in these gardens so you will often see opposites subtly paired. Taoism supported the development of the chemical, medicinal and botanical arts and the practices of meditation and the physical discipline, Tai Chi Ch'uan. Gardens became a place to watch and learn from everything - the rocks, water, fish, animals, and plants.

Chinese Buddhism brought with it the philosophy that through disciplined and persistent effort, one could attain supreme bliss. The entire world is transitory and the key to understanding this is to move beyond the thinking mind. An empty mind brings us beyond ourselves to the connection with everything. With the knowledge that everything is transitory there is also the wisdom that all life is sacred and therefore connection to the natural world is important. The idea is not to withdraw from the world but to infuse our experience of the world with sacred thoughts and feelings.

Plants were cultivated in great reverence for their healing and meditative uses. In fact Ginkgo biloba, thought to be extinct, was found growing in a Japanese Buddhist monastery in 1691. This plant is known to improve memory and is used in treating heart and kidney ailments. Plants were cultivated for tea to be used in meditative practices. The garden was the alchemy that brought together meditation, study of the arts, and the fusion of our inner and outer lives.

The history of the Chinese people and great philosophies helped mold the garden. We can learn much from these spaces and use the framework to help us to create gardens that are beautiful, healthy, and auspicious.

Elements of the Chinese Garden

Throughout Chinese history, gardens were designed from the desire to create a space that helped people find their place in the grand cosmic scheme. Incorporating special symbols, shapes, and elements provided essentials that have deep and long-standing meaning.

China is a land with many beloved and important natural features. Mountains which are considered sacred dominate and surround the country in the four cardinal directions. Three great rivers that run through the country feed the people and the land. Mountains and water have such significance that the word for landscape in China, *Shan Shui*, means "mountains and water." These elements are viewed as living parts of the earth. Rivers are seen as the arteries of the earth's body; water its blood and breath; and mountains its skeleton.

The elements found in the garden were used to recall and bind you to the natural forms of the earth and all of its associations. For instance, in China mountains have always been associated with heaven - a magical but thoroughly accessible place. The rocks symbolizing mountains represent a source of help and joy and are used in the garden to attract good feng shui. Symbolism through rocks, pools, or trees is always present, always intentional, and should always be meaningful to you.

Everything is made of energy and possesses life force so it is incumbent upon us to treat these elements with respect and reverence. Buddha said that each stone possesses a soul and will enter Nirvana.

The use of paired opposites (yin and yang) in Chinese gardens is a strong design principle. Ancient legends ascribed immortality in grottos where mountains and earth come together. Water, the amorphous fluid shape, and rock, the solid hard uplifting shape, are paired to offer contrasts. In other examples, we can also see these types of contrasts where bare walls are interrupted with the beautiful shape of a tree outline and where the sun and the trees cast shadows and light on the ground.

This picture shows the pairing of rocks and water as contrast and the pairing of building and nature as contrast.

Water fits and yields to circumstances as it courses over obstacles yet it will wear away rock. In nature, water may be seen as the still, quiet, reflective lake or the bubbling moving, lively stream flowing over rocks. Water provides charm and variety to the garden. In Chinese gardens water's cooling effects are important to the garden atmosphere and temperatures in the house. The water irrigates the garden. While you may not want to bear the expense and maintenance required by a large water feature such as a lake, a small fountain or pond could produce the beneficial qualities of earth's lifeblood.

Feng Shui, the Home and the Garden

Applying feng shui to the garden can correct imbalances in ch'i that may result from the design of the house. For example, a house may not have been oriented to take advantage of the sun and consequently may be too dark or too light. Houses that shut nature out, or that dominate a site, are also out of equilibrium. An irregularly shaped house will produce missing potential in one's life. Garden plants can be used to "fill in" the missing areas of potential.

Chinese gardens were often set up as a series of small courtyards around the house to maximize a home's interface with the garden. It has often been described as the equivalent to unrolling a landscape scroll. This can provide you with a variety of experiences - viewing rocks, plants and water and even different views of the same landscape scene as you progress through the garden. While you may not have the opportunity to do this, you can maximize your view to the outdoors and create comfortable spaces near and in the garden that you can enjoy. One way to foster movement in the garden would be to design a path or device such as a labyrinth or maze, which can be used for contemplation and can also offer you different views of your garden. Some labyrinths have sacred shapes so when the user walks through the shape, the symbology moves him to contemplate life on a deeper level.

People often ask me whether changes in the garden are less effective than changes in the house. The principle to keep in mind is that the places closest to a person have the greatest influence over the changes. For example, feng shui changes to your bed would have the most influence in your life while changes in the bedroom would be next. Therefore, formal changes in the garden are less likely to affect you as strongly as changes to the places you relate to intimately for longer periods of time. In other words, the farther away from your body the changes occur, the less influence they would exert. However, as the garden has nature on its side, the natural world helps to restore balance just by its own essence. Also, the power of nature balances the house and our hearts while adding extra momentum.

Uses of Plants in the Garden

Our gardens and landscapes can help to deepen our relationship with nature. We can foster this in many ways. For example, we can celebrate the cardinal directions, seasons, and orientation of the sun with compasses, plants, and sundials. Plants can be used to mark changing light in the day and season by the shadows cast in small spaces or against walls. Plants that show the changing seasons can be used to illustrate the passing of time for reflection purposes.

Plants are one of the chief indicators of life force in a location. When considering which plants to include in your garden you should remember not only to choose plants that will thrive in your location, but also to select the color palette that will refresh your heart and delight your senses. The classic Chinese garden was intended as a breeding ground of fantasy and magic. Yours should be, too!

Expressing the seasons in the garden is crucial. Flowering plants in Chinese gardens are not as prolific as those in Western gardens. However, seasons are expressed by emphasizing plants associated with them such as the Peony in spring and early summer, the Lotus in summer, and the Chrysanthemum in autumn. Flowering plants are often placed in pots that can be moved around to allow for the best display and to accommodate the activities of the garden, creating emphasis in the active areas and decreasing distractions in the passive, contemplative areas.

Plants are so significant in Chinese culture that they informally call their country the "Central Flower Kingdom" to signify that they represent the natural order of the universe. We bond with plants when they have sensual or emotional appeal to us. A plant is meaningful to us through an innate, emotional, or learned response. Innate appeals are our primary sensual experiences of a plant, as when we can't get enough of its fragrance. Consider the emotional response in China where the chrysanthemum was developed over centuries to such a degree that many beautiful shapes and colors were cultivated to appeal to the Chinese people's joy and love of them. A learned response occurs when we uncover information about a plant that endears it to us, such as knowing that Sage is good for treating colds and other afflictions.

Observing the characteristics of a plant and how it grows can teach us much about life. In China, plants are used as living metaphors for sought-after qualities or reminders of attributes

The pine represents resilience, integrity, dignity, and longevity.

Bamboo symbolizes fidelity and peace.

to be attained. Symbolism is not an afterthought. It is a primary emotional element of the garden form. For example, plants most associated with Chinese gardens are conifers such as the pines and cedars. These plants remain green during the winter and develop fascinating configurations suggesting tenacity, persistence, and longevity. Their bark is often compared to dragon scales and their roots to dragon claws. These images conjure up the spiritual energy of these powerful mystical animals. Bamboo, another plant often found in Chinese gardens, is strong and resilient. Because it grows rapidly, it is considered a model of self-development. It also grows in measured segments, which shows a sense of limit and propriety, and also in clumps that do not flower, which shows a sense of being part of a clan- working with rather than competing with others.

In early China, a garden was a place where the individual moved beyond their senses. Viewing a garden meant more just watching the bamboo sway in the wind. Seeing the fish move in the water reminded them to emulate the "happiness of the fishes." Fragrance induced clear thinking. Fruit and herbs were an important aspect of the garden. Sound was encouraged not only with water, but also with cicadas, dragonflies, crickets, and frogs. Birds were valued for the melodies that they produced. Music was often played in the garden, which provided another form of auditory delights. Walkways that moved through mountains of stones invited the visitor to touch the stones.

Garden Structures

The Chinese pavilion is the vehicle for shelter where you can create poetry, art, and music. The arts that were expressed in the garden not only were inspired by the garden but also inspired garden designers to incorporate the elements painted or described in art. In the Western world we see the arts inspiring each other in places such as Monet's garden. Bringing the creative arts into the garden is a perfect application for joining arts together to create something greater than a single expression could. For example, some of the most beautiful poetry in China was often written in and about gardens.

Structures in the garden should not be considered intrusive. They show man's presence as an important sign of his part in the cosmic scheme. We fit and belong in the garden. Garden walls in China divide one large space into several smaller spaces. The wall, rather than being a solid mass that makes you feel closed in, has openings to allow for selective views for the next space to give perspective. Patterns for the opening "windows" or "doors" are often fanciful and evocative. Windows can be shaped like circles, fans, vases, and leaves - all meaningful

The shapes of windows on the wall not only add interest from afar but offer interesting views to the garden.

symbols. One classic pattern, cracked ice, symbolizes winter ice breaking as spring approaches. This is a reminder of the joy you can experience upon the renewal of life. The archetypal shape of the moon gate is like a heavenly portal. The circle has always been the symbol for heaven. Interestingly, this transcends the Chinese culture and has been expressed in many spiritual traditions throughout the world.

Walls are often used to signal shifts from one space to the next. This is not only a physical separation, but is also a shift in the purpose or feel of the new space. Outer walls may have an ideograph (a symbol representing a concept) recommending that the household members remember their filial duty, fidelity to family, loyalty to rulers, and sincerity of friends. Inner gateways may have symbols for longevity, riches, happiness and good luck. These ideographs could also indicate your feelings or hopes when you enter the space and can produce vibratory influences beneficial to your family and guests.

Walkways and bridges are often designed in a zigzag manner to discourage bad spirits from following you and to encourage different views of the garden. Many gardens also have a covered structure over the walkway which can be decorated with beautiful painted scenes or embellished with carved wooden shapes.

Ornaments, such as statues and signs and shapes of windows and doors are all used to define the space and set the mood. Rocks may be carved with images of Kuan Yin, the Chinese goddess of mercy, or Amitabha Buddha, a popular object of devotion, but these are usually not stand-alone aspects of the garden. Statues are not usually seen in Chinese gardens. If they are used, they are placed outside of the garden or at the entrance. A classic illustration of this is seen where fu dogs or dragons flank the entry to a house or building. They define one's personal space and let all who enter know that this place is defended. Motifs are often built into the structures around the garden. Handrails, eaves, doors, and windows sport symbols of long life and good luck.

Motifs and Illusions in the Garden

Motifs are often used to set the mood or to adjust the luck in the garden. Sometimes significant animal symbols such as the crane (representing longevity) or the animals of the four directions - white tiger, azure dragon, red phoenix and black tortoise - are used. The bat, for example, symbolizes happiness and may be applied to the latticework in windows and fences or as decoration on overhead structures or on walls facing the garden. Paving may have the cracked ice symbol, plum blossoms, or octagon shapes.

Besides considering motifs to express in your garden, you should consider how the images will be seen when structuring your garden. The placement of these images and how your garden is laid out depends upon three perspectives - from the visitor, home and pavilion.

Cracked ice pattern encourages new beginnings.

Black Tortoise

Classical Chinese garden design incorporates different ways to see a garden: *borrowing, screening,* and *imitating.* A *borrowing view* uses elements from outside the garden and makes it appear as though they are part of your garden. Borrowing views give you "more land" or incorporates something important to add balance or "expand" your property. For a city dweller, the amount of space surrounding a house is often limited. Hiding walls from the viewer can open views to the mountains in the distance and create the illusion that they are included in the owner's land. Bringing views of mountains into the garden invites a heavenly force into your space. You can borrow views from above by having the sky reflected in the water below. This also creates yin-yang balance by bringing the sky into the earth, the ch'i of boundless heaven as a force on earth. Siting pavilions downwind from lotus ponds allows for "borrowing the scent" from the lotus. You use heaven's breath to bring you a wonderful odoriferous experience. Trees from your neighbor's yard, seen from your house, can expand your property in all directions.

The second kind of view is a *screening view.* When the view is partially hidden, it adds a sense of mystery, which can bring delight and surprise to the viewer. An example of this can be a Chinese screen, a wall, or a moon gate that lets you see part of the view and uses your curiosity to invite you to what is hidden. When you wind a path around shrubs or trees in the garden, it can call you to the unknown. Rock formations, trees, and vines can partially veil or frame buildings and views.

See how the larger landscape is micro-scoped in the smaller landscape. This garden is borrowing from the larger landscape and illustrates bringing yang into yin. It is also bringing the heaven of mountain to the house. Also here you are seeing only part of the garden so your imagination can go wild about the rest.

The third type of view is an *imitating view*. This view uses an image that reminds you of a powerful symbol. For instance, when a rock in your garden looks like a turtle, you may be inviting longevity - the turtle's symbolism. Another example might be a serpentine wall that resembles a dragon. Since dragons represent good luck and protection, imagine having your property surrounded by that image.

Traditional Chinese gardens also have three basic functions. They need to be *walk-able* so that you can amble through them, *viewable* so that you can see them from different angles in different places, and *habitable* so people have a presence in the garden.

As a new garden designer you may want to consider these principles as a checklist after you have decided on your basic garden concept. Some gardens don't have all of these elements, but they add can charm and allure to the garden so I recommend that you think about them as you consider the next group of design principles.

Chinese Design Principles

The essence of Chinese garden design is balance. The components of balance are *yin-yang balance, completion, symmetry, proportion, change, movement, boundaries* and *centers*. These are the same principles that landscape architects use today. As it will take time to master these ideas, start by looking for them as you view gardens to assess whether each element is successful (whether or not they please you). If a garden doesn't have all the principles, note if it feels as though something is missing.

Throughout this book I will discuss *yin-yang balance*. Many people see yin and yang as separate and opposite principles, but they are actually dependent on each other for definition in much the same way that we cannot define tall without short, light without dark, or old without young. The idea in landscape design is to have balance. Whether visible or invisible, we always seek balance. Some of my clients just love lavender gardens. I don't discourage their desire for subtle color, but I will often suggest that equilibrium be brought about through brightly colored foliage to highlight a balanced composition. If you don't want color in the garden you may express yin-yang balance in other ways. You may have an extremely open exposed area and balance it with a shady glen nearby. This also means hard textures such as rocks could have soft textures such as ferns near them. Big-leafed plants, such as an Umbrella Tree can be balanced with small-leafed plants, such as the delicate China Doll. A subtle option would be showing yin and yang together, such as capturing the yang of heaven in the yin of earth with a pond.

You can see how important *completion* is when we are placing the Ba-Gua on a property or a house. A missing area could cause missing potential in an important aspect of your life. Likewise within a landscape, the composition needs to convey a sense of wholeness. The walls or plants that form the borders of the garden and the internal garden composition should combine to create a feeling of perfection realized. Even when you are leading the viewer to other spaces, the composition must have a sense of the whole. The most common lack of completion I see is in public spaces where you see a center but no edges. These spaces are often empty because people feel unsafe without some sense of enclosure. A hillside home that has a totally unobstructed view, without a hint of boundary, often feels as if you will fall off the edge.

Chinese gardens are designed with a strong sense of *symmetry*- but not the perfect symmetry of the formal French garden. The Chinese view is that perfect symmetry is unrefined. Sometimes asymmetry is hidden in visual symmetry-a pair of lions, one male and the other female, guarding an entrance. Another form of symmetry, which is often more desirable, would be asymmetrical balance. When you see this type of symmetry, you see a complete composition as well as a complete balance.

See the asymmetrical balance where the rock balances the tree, not only composing a complete picture but also juxtaposing the yang rock against the yin tree.

Proportion should always be adequate and rhythmic. No element should overshadow another element. They should balance each other. There should be a rhythm to the composition so your eyes keep moving and exploring the scene as you see new aspects of balance with each viewing. Proportion should allow for humans to fit into the space. If you have ever been in a miniature replica of a city you know how it feels to be too large for a space. If you have been in a huge palace or public space, such as a museum, you might have experienced the uncomfortable feeling of being dwarfed by the space.

Change is a delightful part of the surprise of a garden. Yearly change happens as plants grow and fill in, or die and are removed. Seasonally, I like to design a garden as if it were an orchestra. Each season highlights a different part of the garden. Autumn Sage, while just another green plant in the summer, becomes ablaze with hummingbird food in the fall. Likewise, daily change is seen as different parts of the garden are highlighted when the sun moves across the sky. At night white flowering plants shine in the moon. Much of the wonder of a garden is opening your eyes to yearly, seasonal, and daily changes which awaken your innocent eyes anew.

Movement is fluidity in the design in contrast to stagnation. If you refer to the above picture you can see that although it is an arrangement of elements intended to fill in a corner, it has movement, not only in the juxtaposition of the rocks and plants, but also in the way it imposes itself on the hard surface. In a Zen rock garden, which may seem stark by many standards, you can see movement in the raked sand. Even the character of rocks expresses

There is no doubt where the center is.

movement when viewed at different angles. Movement in a garden can become more literal as you move along a path or walkway through the space.

The entry to a garden marks the beginning of the space while the walls or trees mark the *boundaries*. Boundaries can be heavy and strong, such as walls and buildings, or softer like trees, or less defined like shrubs. Layered shrubs, with larger ones in the back and smaller ones in front can soften the feel of the boundary. Outside land forms, such as hills and mountains, also may form boundaries.

The *center* of a garden is its heart and carries the feeling, theme, mood, or the power of the space. It does not have to be located in the physical center. The center should have a solid feel and represent a pivotal part of the garden. It should draw your attention and make you feel good about the about the role it plays in your space. It can be a surprise or represent something a bit different, but it shouldn't be out of context with the rest of your design. A statue is used to create a center in some Western gardens; however, in Chinese gardens a lone statue represents that the owner can become trapped in his house or isolated in another place like jail. Thus, a lone statue or tree should be avoided.

Here a lone statue is a prisoner.

The elements fight for center, creating confusion.

In reviewing the history, philosophy, and forms that are used in Chinese gardens, the one underlying theme is the meaning. Everything in the garden should have personal significance to the user. It should tie the past, in forms and philosophies, into the present garden structure, and project the hopes for the future with the meaning of the objects used. Many of us don't have the history of the Chinese culture, but we have the freedom to adopt meaningful ideas, objects, and designs from their culture and our own to create a garden that will embody and reflect meaning to us.

In the chapters that follow you will see many different ways to accentuate the meaning in your garden. The next chapter will discuss the types of cures that could be used in your garden to help you to assess your life's goals.

Chapter 4

The Forces Affecting Our Lives

When creating a garden within an artificially formed location like our properties, we need to assess the conditions created by artificial structures and boundaries. Feng shui garden design helps us understand the forces around us and use principles and creativity to balance our environments. In doing so, we restore our lives to a harmonious relationship with the earth.

Seeing the garden in terms of feng shui offers us new design ideas for our gardens. Garden design in general has moved toward less formal and more "natural" shapes and materials. Natural shapes and materials help us to step outside the order of our regularly shaped houses and welcome the chaos and wild beauty found in nature. Restoring the balance between our houses and gardens is accomplished through the principles we have explored and will further examine in this chapter: ch'i, yin and yang, the five elements, and others.

The Trail of Ch'i

Do you think you have a brown thumb? Do you have problems with plants that seem to wilt or die? Energy affects you and everything in the environment. In places where ch'i is flowing well, the land is green and lush, plants look hearty and abundant, and people who inhabit the area are healthy and prosperous. A location where ch'i is not flowing well may have infertile or toxic soil, dead or dying plants, and people who have many life problems. Problems with ch'i will affect different people according to the type of blockage or lack, the location of the ch'i problem, and the individual and their particular fate.

When I was first introduced to the concept of ch'i I was intimidated by the responsibility of understanding where and how energy flows. I found that using the metaphors of water and wind made it easier for me to picture exactly how energy moves through a space. Energy will be obstructed wherever wind, water, or a human is blocked or diverted. We can see this in action when we look at the ocean or a river.

As ocean interfaces with the water's edge the water moves easily where channels gently guide its movement. Notice how vibrant flowing water is. It seems to enliven us just looking at it. Where water hits rocks, they are eroded and worn down. Where there are obstacles not only is there erosion but the areas behind the rock or obstacle become dead space. This is what happens to energy flowing throughout your environment daily.

There will be many solutions suggested here for problematic situations. When you ask for help, you start the movement toward change. Many clients have called me to do feng shui work on their homes, businesses, and gardens thinking that my mere presence there will fix all of their ills. Just reading a book or employing a feng shui expert will not fix your problems. Your work and sincere effort to change the feng shui must be done. Nothing happens without your active participation.

The objective of balancing our environment is that we can control the directions of our lives. Of course this is not 100 percent. Fate or destiny does play a part in our future but we can affect much more of our lives than we ever dreamed using feng shui. When life throws us a curve as it inevitably does, we have ways to learn from the experience and move on. The more we learn about ourselves and the way energy in its many forms flows, the more power we have to affect our lives.

Sometimes the changes that have come as a result of the cures are unanticipated. Often our view of what is best for us is too limited. One of my clients who wanted a committed relationship from the man she was seeing was rudely jilted within three days of our consultation. She is now in a committed relationship with a man who, unlike the person she was with when we did the consultation, is more suited to her.

The Nine Cures for Your Landscape

These cures or enhancements are reintroduced here with further uses. As we review specific situations you will have a better idea of how these solutions are applied.

Mundane	Transcendental
1. Light-producing elements:	
Mirrors - Convex mirrors allow safe views	Deflect negative energy Expand energy to draw from many directions
Concave mirrors	Turn energy on its head, negating a negative force
Ba-Gua mirrors	Deflect negative energy
Crystals - Add interest to the garden	Deflect negative energy,
	Attract positive energy.
Lighting - Lights up dark yards.	Positively shifts energy, decreases stagnation.
2. Sound-producing elements:	
Wind chimes - Provide beautiful sound to enhance your garden space	Attract good energy, especially at the front entry
Bells - Create beautiful sound	Balance an irregular house shape
Music - Masks unpleasant sounds	Increase overall ch'i
Birds and bees - Pollinators of our plants	See Chapter 7 for further discussion
3. Life force elements:	
Fish - Watching fish lowers blood pressure Pets - Focus of our love in the environment Wild animals - Bring in the chaos of nature	See Chapter 7 for further discussion
Bonsai - Good in small gardens, focal points	Conceptual idea -less excels over more, seeing macro through microcosm
Plants - Provide for our needs – food, clothing, shelter, oxygen	Used to complete spaces & bring Ba-Gua colors into landscape

4. Weight and heavy objects:	
Statues/sculptures -Provide beauty, delight, meaning & focal points	Stabilize energy and draw energy of the object for instance, Buddha statue draws meditative quality
Rocks - Provide variety, elevation, interest	Heavy element -provides stability to any area; symbolizes heaven
Walls - Provide separation of spaces;	Deflects negative energy; motifs on boundary walls and gateways provide meaning for space
5. Color:	
All colors serve to enliven & set the mood	Attract energy for the space according to the element they represent e.g. pink for relationship of Ba-Gua area
Other color sequences	Used for special transcendental cures e.g. rainbow colors can greatly increase the ch'i.
6. Moving objects:	
Wind mills, mobiles, whirligigs - Provide excitement, focal point	Enliven ch'i; deflect or attract energy; lift energy brings harmony in a garden
7. Water elements:	
Water sculptures/fountains Provide focus	Flowing water symbolizes money &
Bird baths - Add water	Calms the ch'i & attracts wildlife
8. Fire producing objects:	
Barbecues and Fireplace or pit - Provide ambiance & a gathering spot	Increase ch'i and deflect negative energy
Others: Discussed in detail later.	

Three Secret Reinforcement

The Three Secret Reinforcement is a ceremony or blessing that is used whenever a cure or enhancement is put into place. A modern day psychologist may say that with this ceremony you are selecting an object to signal your intention for change. Whenever I see a cure that I have blessed, I am reminded of my vision of its purpose. A sociologist may say that ceremonies and blessings always have been used to help people to lay claim to and connect with their land. Indigenous societies everywhere conduct ceremonies to bond them to the land, their activities, and possessions of everyday life. A holy person may view the blessing and ceremony as a means to create sacred surroundings. This would be my favorite explanation. Whatever explanation is given, the use of the ceremony and the consequence of doing a ceremony every time we put an object into place is that the effectiveness of the cure is increased by 100 to 120 percent. In fact, for a cure to work, faith and sincerity are the most important components. Once you have done this ritual, it doesn't need to be repeated.

The Three Secret Reinforcement has the three following components:

1. **BODY SECRET**: Use ritual hand gestures ("mudras") to involve the body in the ceremony.

   One example of this is the mudra the Heart Calming Mudra, which is the right hand over the left with palms facing up and the tips of the thumbs touching. Many people also use the prayer gesture of palms placed together in front of the heart.

2. **SPEECH SECRET**: A prayer or mantra recited nine times. This gives voice to your intention. Examples of this are:

   Heart Calming Mantra: Gate, gate, para gate, para sum gate, Bodhi so ha.

   Six True Words: Om Ma Ni Pad Me Hum.

   Others: From your religion or spiritual tradition.

3. **MIND SECRET**: Visualization and mystic intent.

   This is your intention, wish, or prayer for the outcome of the situation. Get as specific as you can and be generous with your hopes and dreams.

The Three Essential Ch'i s

There are essentially three types of ch'i that affect us all. The ch'i of atmosphere can be seen by the sun, stars, moon, and other heavenly bodies. This is the energy of heaven and is both seen and unseen. We see the sun, moon, and stars but don't see black holes, sun spots, and what happens in outer space. The atmosphere causes tides, typhoons, rainstorms, droughts, and airplane accidents. The second essential ch'i is of the earth. It is what provides us with our home. As I have said before we can judge the ch'i of the land by viewing whether plants are living or dying and sense whether it is a spot that feels good. The third essential ch'i is that of man. Human ch'i is seen on an individual level, a family level, a societal level, and a national level.

Yin and Yang in the Garden

If we understand how to balance yin and yang in our garden, we will know how to relate to our environment in a harmonious manner. As we view nature without man's intercession, we see the practice of yin and yang balancing each other and ever changing. On the macro scale, this process is the building up and the eroding of mountains. On the micro scale it is the automatic balance of colors and textures in a wildflower garden. On our properties, we can use our knowledge of yin and yang to make additional adjustments to the imbalances of our land. In our gardens we can create this balance mindfully using the yin and yang principles to design natural-looking beauty in our landscape. When you implement feng shui in your garden you

Yin/Yang can be expressed as soft shapes against a structured architecture, upward vs. falling leaves, hot vs. cool colors and many other ends of the continuum.

bring balance to the land and your life. You don't need to implement every cure or change every space on your land; only change the areas out of balance through cures and enhancements.

The garden itself is a statement of the yin-yang balance, using undulating natural forms to balance the straight geometrical lines of the home or building. Within the garden, the most pleasing compositions are those where there is a balance of bold and fine textures, dark and light colors, shadows and light, tall and flat forms, active and passive spaces, open and enclosed spaces, regularly shaped plants and asymmetric shapes, quiet and noisy spaces.

I often design landscapes that achieve this balance only to return later and find a plant overgrown or missing and the composition is destroyed. As the landscape matures the original design must change as trees grow and produce more shade or die and open areas up to the sun. Unlike the home, where you move a piece of furniture and the balance is established, conditions in the garden are ever-changing. You must always be aware of changes to maintain the balance of the garden.

Expressing and balancing yin and yang in the garden is an important design principle. Part of the decision about shapes, colors, sizes, and textures will be based on judgment and intuition. The shape, size, and texture may shift these elements to the other side.

Yin	Yang
Flat, smooth rocks	Craggy, jagged rocks
Serene, quiet pond	Fountain or bubbling water feature
Overgrown leafy plants	Plants with a strong structure or few leaves
Concrete or gray, dark, smooth paving	Bright, sandy, rough-textured paving
Curving forms	Straight lines
Fine-textured plants such as Yew, Fir, Fern Pine	Bold-textured plants such as Bird of Paradise, Common Horsechestnut, Magnolia
Weeping shapes such as Willow, Weeping Birch	Projective shape such as Italian Cypress, Olive, English Hawthorn, Redbud
Sunken lawn or garden area	Light fixtures, barbecues
Dark shadowy cool areas	Bright, hot areas
Planted areas	Paved areas

It is useful to see yin and yang as opposing pairs for the sake of understanding how to create balance in the design of the garden but the two are more on a continuum. The more extreme the example of a yin or yang element will require a strong element to balance it.

For example, if the paving adjacent to our home is a bright, rough-textured sandstone (yang) we can compensate with a large expanse of lawn (weak yin) or one large canopy shade tree (strong yin).

The same principles hold true with shadows and light. When a shade tree provides a dappled light, there usually is a perfect balance of yin and yang. Dense trees create dim light which may only allow for a white flowering plant such as impatiens to balance the yin. We may want to use a dense tree on the south or a sun-exposed area while a sparse or open canopy tree might be the preferred choice for the north side of the house where the sun is at a premium.

The colors we choose to use also express the yin and yang forces. Colors have a dramatic and substantial effect on people who interact with them daily. I have made the mistakes of every amateur gardener who falls in love with one plant or color and throws the balance of the garden off. In the Knowledge area of my garden, I was so delighted finding blue plants, I soon created a very subdued area in the front of my property. It wasn't until bright yellow daffodils came up in the spring that I realized how much they were needed to balance the yin in that area.

The bright, hot colors on the color wheel, the reds, oranges, and yellows, are generally yang colors while the cool colors such as the greens, blues, and purples are generally yin colors. While most people favor one spectrum or another, it is important to create the balance between the hot and cool colors. If a client is partial to the hot colors, I suggest adding some cool colors such as purple or blue to balance. Conversely, when a client loves the cool range, I recommend balancing with a touch of yellow or red to lift the energy. Where these choices are not viable, I recommend using white or gray-colored plants that can tone down the hot colors or lift the energy of the cool colors.

Selecting Rocks for Your Garden

Rocks are important to include in the landscape if it is feasible. Rocks can be used for their symbolism, such as the Chinese connection to the heavenly forces or for the feeling of stability that they provide. Rocks are often paired with water for the yin-yang balance. They may be used also as a piece of sculpture. To choose rocks:

1. Determine the use of a rock or grouping of rocks.

    a. Meditative purposes.

    b. To pair with a water feature.

    c. To punctuate and add variety to the landscape.

    d. To add a particular quality that you desire.

    e. To stabilize a part of your life.

    f. To mimic a mountain.

2. Find rocks that will suit your purpose. Many people have made exacting arts of selecting rocks. Your best guide for selecting a rock is your emotional reaction to it. If it "makes your heart sing" you should have it in your garden.

   a. For meditative purposes, some people love to use rocks that are complex, with crags and twists that remind them of the many complexities of life. Others prefer smooth, regular shapes to represent the calmness that they want to attract into their lives. Smooth rocks may also represent how life evens out our imperfections.

   b. To group rocks around a water feature, you may use rocks that are seen near rivers or waterfalls in the area. If the water feature is highly architectural or used near the house, you may use rocks whose color and character meld with your house style. When designing rocks in a water feature, include three rocks of different heights either inside the pond or to the rear of the pond.

   c. Rocks that punctuate and add variety to your landscape are best selected from indigenous rocks that relate to the colors and textures in your environment.

   d. Some people want to use particular rocks that have long-standing significance to them or their culture. For instance, Chinese culture has held that jade is a symbol of supreme excellence and purity. This token may be used in the Ba-Gua area that this quality is needed.

   e. Feng shui placement has other uses for rocks. They are used to create stability in specific areas and are used to "weight down" areas that are geographically high or out of balance. It can also create stability in an aspect of life. For instance, if your finances are always up and down, rocks can help to bring you stability and peace in that area.

   f. To use rocks that mimic mountains find rocks similar to the indigenous rock or rock reminiscent of your favorite mountains.

   g. Rocks in Chinese gardens often take on particular forms because it is thought that without form the ch'i will be static or stuck. This is particularly true if there is just one rock. If the rock takes on the form of a lion, turtle, or frog or has holes in it, the ch'i can flow through. This way the rock takes on a powerful life force.

Pairing rocks and water in the garden is another opportunity to play with yin and yang. Besides the forms that can be either yin or yang depending on whether you are viewing them as uplifting and yielding or active and passive, rocks and water have a deeper effect on our psyche. Like the placement of a building, the locating of rocks and water is a permanent and stationary event. Because they are unchanging, they provide a focus for our attention that quiets our nature and links us to an interconnection with all things.

Selecting Water for Your Garden.

Whenever I suggest that a client add a water feature, the reaction is always one of delight. Few people are not fascinated and delighted by the presence of water. I am always left to wonder why everyone doesn't already have a water feature in his or her life!

1. Determine the purpose for water.

    a. Used to create harmony for a particular area such as the entry.

    b. For auditory pleasure. When placing for the sound find the place that it will add the widest range of use. Maybe it is placed between the center of the garden and the house so that it may be enjoyed inside as well as outside.

    c. As a home for plants and animals.

    d. As a still, absorbing element. This may be used for contemplation or as a feng shui adjustment for an overactive area or person.

    e. All of the above.

2. The type of water feature you choose will depend on other factors. Most water features can be arranged to accommodate the above needs. Factors to consider are:

    a. Money you have to invest in this feature.

    b. Space to build the feature.

    c. Time and energy to maintain the feature.

3. Various types of water features.

    a. Ready-made fountain bought from a store. This could be a tabletop size that you place at the front door. Be sure that you have an electrical hook up available.

    b. Small barrel or bowl fountain either ready-made or one that you build from a "how to" book.

    c. Pond and/or waterfall feature. You or a contractor can construct this. If you want to incorporate fish and plants, it will need to be 18 inches deep, minimum, and have some type of filtration system.

If your choice of water feature is a fishpond, it needs to be carefully located. Any water feature will require information and dedication on your part. There are many good books about building and maintaining ponds. Here are a few tips:

If plants are going to be used, a place that has six to eight hours of sun per day is desirable. Four hours of light is minimal.

As with plants in the garden, there are many beautiful, flowering and fragrant plants that can be used in a pond. The composition of the plants in a pond can be interesting and varied.

To receive fish, a pond should be at least 18 inches deep and koi should have at least 24 inches. Some municipalities will require security fencing around the area if the pond is 24 inches or deeper.

There are many "ready-made" pond liners that are less costly than a concrete pool.

If you want a waterfall or fountain you will need a pump and electricity.

Locate the pond where you can watch the activity in it. Birds, dragonflies, and other creatures will be drawn to the pond.

Be prepared to spend time maintaining the pond. Leaf drop from trees and shrubs will need to be cleaned, algae removed, and it will require attention to maintain the balance of the various elements.

Balancing Yourself and Your Garden

Aren't we all just seeking to bring a balance to our lives? Some people will answer that they will worry about balance and harmony as soon as they have enough money to make the rent or to buy the new car. Others want the relationship of their dreams; some people only want to repair relationships with their children or their parents. The fact is that wanting these "material" goals is righting the imbalance within you. By adjusting the feng shui you can foster the energy to bring about these changes in your life.

Balancing all of the elements of the environment is the eternal challenge of the designer. To meet this challenge requires the most important and difficult part of design, using your intuition. Relying on intuition requires a sense of trust of your instincts and a constant awareness of your surroundings. I wasn't born or taught to maintain this trust and awareness but I have been able to learn to create balance and harmony in my environment and to be observant of when things slip out of balance. Working in the garden and meditating has helped teach me to stay conscious and aware in the moment. Making mistakes and learning from them has also taught me well.

Balancing the yin and yang in our garden will not only balance our land but also parts of our personalities. If you identify with some negative aspects of the yin or yang personality, you will create more balance by increasing the other aspect. For instance, if you tend to be moody and depressed, you may want to have more orange flowers in your garden or a bubbly fountain. If you are on the go all the time and wearing yourself out, you may want to add a bench, soft pink, purple, and blue flowers or a quiet, still body of water to calm your active energy. Remember that plants don't have to be in bloom to provide the energy for balance. Their essence and potential is providing the balancing force. Adding these balancing elements may not feel comfortable because change is unfamiliar. Some people prefer to start slowly and add color in small steps. Making changes slowly is a good idea not only to get used to the change aesthetically but also to observe the effect of the change in your life. The idea behind creating a change is to direct your life toward a more balanced future. Often when we don't take on these challenges ourselves, life has a way of creating them for us. I have often seen an overactive achiever become ill, which forces them to stop and rest. If you can proactively make the space for restorative time, your body may not need to create illness.

The Five Elements Energy and Design

The five elements of water, wood, fire, earth, and metal are also used to analyze your land and to bring it into balance. As previously mentioned, the five elements are forces of energy derived from yin and yang. The relationship of the five elements to each other and their placement within the Ba-Gua can help us determine if an area is deficient or has an excess of a particular element which requires correction. As with yin and yang, the qualities of each element such as shapes, colors, seasons, times, and directions are used to help us balance and correct any shortcomings.

Water has the characteristics of a fluid, downward movement. Its movement is gentle. Water's season is winter and the time of day is midnight. Water represents the shift from yin of the evening to the coming yang of the day. The sense related to water is that of hearing. Water can be dynamic and flowing like a river or the ocean responding to the pull of the moon or static like a well, pool, or lake. In our landscapes, water is represented by an amorphous shape and the color black - could be the curves in our lawn or walkways. The right amount adds pleasant flow to the design composition. Too little of the flowing element may create areas that seem stagnant. Too much of the water element seems disorganized, as if energy is flowing in too many directions.

Wood's energy is of upward growth and movement. It moves expansively in all directions. Wood's season is spring and the time of day is mid-morning. This energy is the promise of the new day in all of its glory. The shape that represents wood is tall and thin like a tree trunk and the color is green. Sight is the sense related to wood. In our landscapes, trees and posts for our porches, gazebos, and overhead structures represent wood. The right amount of wood provides shade and variation to the landscape design. Too little wood element makes our landscape flat and featureless. Too much wood produces too much structure and a crowded, dense feeling.

Fire is an explosive, hot, consuming energy. Its movement is upward and expansive. Fire's season is summer and the time of day is noon, when the fullness of the day (yang) begins to decline (yin). This is the energy of the peak of the cycle, the height of beauty. The shape of fire is pointed like a flame and the color is red. The sense related to fire is the sense of taste. In our landscapes, pointed roofs or plants might represent fire. The right amount of fire produces excitement, clarity, and attraction. Too little fire creates a lack of stimulation and seems dull. Too much fire produces a chaotic, uncomfortable, and threatening feeling to the landscape.

Earth is a firm, reliable energy. It is stable, but not stagnant. It is in the central point between all of the energies and is represented by the season of late summer and late afternoon. The sense related to earth is the sense of touch. The shape associated with earth is flat or square and its color is yellow. In our landscape earth is seen in our paving or walls. The right amount of earth provides stability and calm. Too little earth produces an insubstantial and weak feeling to the landscape composition. Too much earth will make the landscape stagnant and uninteresting.

Metal is a contracting and heavy energy. Its movement is inward. Metal's season is the autumn and time of day is evening. The shape associated with metal is rounded or dome-shaped and the color is white. The sense of smell is the sense related to metal. Rounded arbors would represent a metal energy in the landscape. The right amount of metal provides a sense of purity and a sturdy, organized quality to the landscape arrangement. Too little metal lacks a sense of charm and grace in the landscape design. Too much metal makes the landscape feel artificial, cute, or sterile.

The elements have natural relationships to each other that can be used to foster balance and enhance our life situations. The cycles of these elements are shown in Ill. 4-1.

The creative cycle shows the natural way one energy element feeds or nurtures the next. In balance, water feeds wood, allowing it to grow. Wood feeds fire by building it. Fire's ashes feed the earth, enriching it. Earth produces Metal. Metal attracts and condenses Water.

Another cycle used to bring an element into balanced relationships is called the controlling cycle. In this cycle, water extinguishes fire, fire melts metal, metal pierces or chops wood, wood depletes earth, and earth blocks water.

Each of these forces can be manipulated using either the controlling cycle or the creative for its maximum effect in our lives. If any element is too strong or too weak, it will be to the detriment of the people living in the space. This is why you need to assess the dynamics of these elements to create a balance and harmony in your garden.

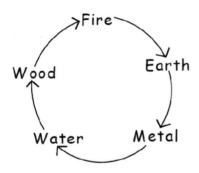

Ill. 4-1 Creative Cycle

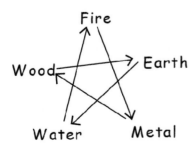

Ill 4-2 Controlling Cycle

When an element is out of balance, we can use the information from these cycles to reestablish balance.

Suppose you have a barbecue in the Children's or metal area. This could support over activity in your children or the child part of your personality because fire melts metal. To compensate or adjust the energy, you could add a fountain to contain the fire (water puts out fire), which, practically speaking, adds a harmonious element that quiets down the hyperactivity.

The Nature of the Five Elements

There is a temptation to make use of the elements literally in the landscape because we are so familiar with the elements. For instance, some of my clients are tempted to place their fire pits in the Fame area even when it is too far from the house for convenience. This can be done but it is so much richer to look at all of the associations that an element has so that we can use any number of options to adjust the landscape. The shapes associated with each are free-form or amorphous for water, tall and thin like a tree for wood, pointed for fire, rectangular or square for earth, and round or oval like a coin for metal. There are examples of each of these shapes both in the built and natural in the landscape. The water shape is found in most of our vines that grow forming themselves to whatever will support them or in free-form lawns or the patterns formed by naturalized daffodils. Wood shape is seen in our columnar-shaped plants or trees such as Italian Cypress or posts for overhead structures. Fire shape is seen in plants such as New Zealand Flax or our picket fences. Earth shape is seen in the stability of flat rocks and in flat groundcovers such as Wild Strawberry. The metal element is seen in round plants and the arch of an arbor.

Another important aspect of an element is its color. The color for water is black, for wood is green, for fire is red, for earth is yellow, and for metal is white. We can find all of these colors in plants commonly used in our landscape and all of the various elements that we add to our gardens such as rocks, water features, paving, walls, pots, and structures.

Finally, using the element itself is often the easiest to think of when we are looking to create balance. In addition to a water feature, water is also represented by glass, mirrors, and free-form art pieces. Columns, plants, and dining tables and chairs represent wood. Fire is represented by lighting and animal life and found in fireplaces and barbecues. Earth is represented by brick, ceramics, rocks, and stones. Metal is represented by arches and found in metal furniture and fencing.

Representations of the Five Elements in the Landscape

Water	*Wood*	*Fire*	*Earth*	*Metal*
Amorphous	Columnar	Pointed	Flat	Rounded or Arched
Black	Green or Blue	Red	Yellow	White
North	East	South	Center	West
Winter	Spring	Summer	Center	Autumn
Kidney	Liver	Heart	Spleen	Lung
Bladder	Gallbladder	Small Intestine	Stomach	Large Intestine
Glass	Plants	Animals	Ceramics	Metal Furniture
Hearing	Sight	Taste	Touch	Smell
Mercury	Jupiter	Mars	Saturn	Venus

Balancing elements is an important part of good landscape design and well-adjusted ch'i. When we see a landscape dominated by one form or element, it is uncomfortable and needs to change. For instance, on properties that are overwhelmed by many large trees (wood element), we can reduce the scale by using a metal arched entry or a metal sculpture to bring the focus away from the overshadowing elements. White flowering or round-shaped plants could also perform the adjustment.

Suppose we live near a huge mountain that has a pointed top (fire element) or across from an imposing building with a pointed roof. Here we can add water elements such as fountains, free-form shaped pathways or lawn lines, glass block embedding in walls, or plants that produce black berries.

On the plains where there are vast flat earth forms (earth element), we can add wood elements such as trees, wood fencing, or decks. Other choices are the use of strong columns in overhead structures or evergreen plants.

If metal or white-colored buildings surround our house (metal element) we can add the fire elements such as carefully placed angled walkways, pointed roofed gazebos, or red flowering or berried plant materials.

These elements and relationships will have further significance when you identify their place in the Ba-Gua.

Another Look at the Ba-Gua

So far we have looked at everything in separate parts to distill the complex information about this ancient philosophy. The beauty and complexity of feng shui analysis lies in the interrelation of ch'i, yin and yang, the five elements, and the Ba-Gua. In reviewing the Ba-Gua again it will be clear how all of these aspects come together.

Each of the Guas is innately yin or yang. According to the *I Ching*, the Guas shown on the bottom side of the Ba-Gua, Ch'i en (Helpful People or Benefactors), K'an (Career), Ken (Knowledge) and Chen (Family) are yang elements. The rest of the Guas, Sun (Wealth), Li (Fame), K'un (Marriage or Partnership), and Tui (Children) are yin elements. In the landscape it is important that the balance of yin and yang elements is evident.

The five elements are specific to five of the Guas. Water is the element for K'an, the Career Gua; wood is the element for Chen, the Family Gua; fire is the element for Li, the Fame Gua; earth is found in the center; and metal is the element for Tui, the ChildrenGua. We can see how elegant and balanced this is when we see that the elements are balanced in relationship to the yin and yang, two elements are yin, two are yang, and one is both. All four sides and the center are represented.

As you recall, the five elements have a natural relationship between them and when we look at the Ba-Gua we see how that can play itself out in the landscape. Suppose we have an imposing pool in our area of Li, Fame which could have the effect of dampening the acknowledgment of our good work in the world. We could add an earth element such as terracotta pots to control the water element in an inauspicious placement.

The Ba-Gua energies, like yin and yang and the five elements, have additional aspects that are important to use in adjusting the energy of the Gua. You may remember from Chapter 2 (see ill. 2-1) that there are colors associated with each area of the Ba-Gua. The colors are consistent with the five elements in the Guas that are represented by elements: black for the Career/Water Gua, green for the Family/Wood Gua, red for the Fame/Fire Gua, yellow for Center/ Earth and white for the Children/ Metal Gua. Likewise, each of the other areas of the Ba-Gua have colors associated with them. The Helpful People area is gray, Knowledge area uses blue, Wealth area is purple and Marriage or Partnership is pink.

Applying the Ba-Gua to the land is relatively simple as was illustrated in Chapter 2. It is also important to know how to apply the Ba-Gua to the home in order to search for extensions or missing parts. We can then use landscape design to fix deficits resulting from missing parts of the house. The Ba-Gua is applied to the house the same way it is applied to the property, (see ill. 2-2 and 2-3). The Ken-K'an-Ch'i en side of the Ba-Gua is laid across the architectural front of the house so that the front door will occur through one of those three Guas.

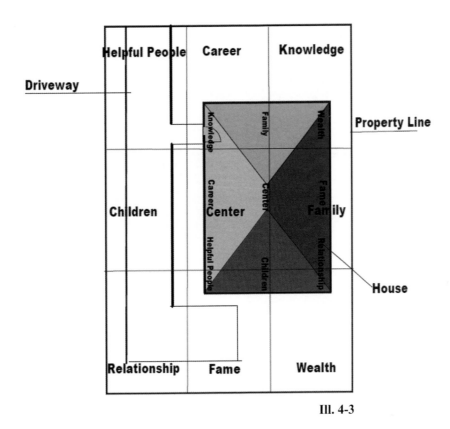

Ill. 4-3

Sometimes my students are confused when the front door of a house is not oriented toward the street. Illustration 4-3 shows a lot where ch'i enters through the Benefactors or Helpful People area, and the front door is in the Children's area of the lot. As we apply the Ba-Gua for the house, the house is entered through the Knowledge area.

The next illustration, Ill. 4-4 shows the property entrance in the Knowledge area and though the front door is in the Family property area, the house is entered through the Career area. In this example the property has an extension in the Relationship area and the house has a missing part in the Knowledge area.

What might be done to balance the missing part of the house Knowledge area? There are many obvious choices. An overhead structure could be built to complete the area with a wind chime hung to attract and complete the energy. A blue flowering or colored tree could be added to the empty space. Nine blue flowering plants could fill in the Knowledge portion. A statue

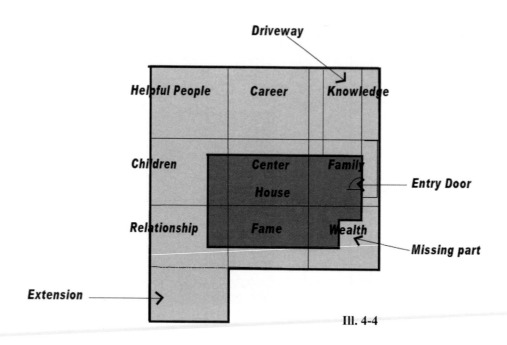

Ill. 4-4

of a scholarly figure could be placed there. A plant known in Chinese culture for scholarly application such as a banana tree could be placed there. Much of the fun of designing using feng shui comes from applying innovative solutions to potential problems.

It is exciting and sometimes daunting to contemplate all of the possibilities for incorporating these ideas in the garden. How does one make sense of which elements to use and where to place them? In the next chapter, we will learn about the many options that can be used in each area of the Ba-Gua.

Chapter 5

Planting the Seeds

We have introduced many concepts for analyzing the feng shui garden. Where do we go from here? How are the tools applied to the land? While those answers will be different for each property, this chapter will offer specific elements, plants, and materials which can be considered in each area of your garden.

To determine which options to use in your garden is to assess the choices and to only do things that will "fit" with your home, land, and aesthetic sensibilities. Use your intuition or that sense of joy to decide what is best.

Creating a garden with feng shui balance is not about using every suggestion. It is about exploring where the imbalances occur either in the Ba-Gua or in your life situations. If there are imbalances, that is where you should begin to change or add to the garden. But you don't need to only follow the suggestions for the plants and elements recommended for a particular Gua area and nothing else. You may have better ideas.

Applying Feng Shui on Your Property

This is where you get to work on the landscape design for your property. Applying the Ba-Gua to your property will involve several steps. The property and home will need to be analyzed to determine what is there and what is missing. You will need to identify your goals and list any weaknesses in yourself that you want to improve. The process can begin by moving step by step through this chapter. Once you complete the analysis you can start the lists of plants, materials, and elements for each area. If this seems intimidating, remember that every designer feels nervous when beginning the process. Later on we will look at this procedure with detailed examples to help you further understand the way it works.

Let's dip back to previous chapters to get some help.

Step 1. Using the sketch or plan of your property described in Chapter 2 (Applying the Ba-Gua to Land), the first step is to analyze your property. Some properties don't have large enough landscape areas to do much of anything. Some properties will have missing parts. There is a whole world of possibilities.

Using the Ba-Gua, determine whether there are any missing or additional areas on your property and then on your house.

Note which areas of the Ba-Gua any problems occur and note the colors and elements that are potential solutions.

Step 2. Use the list "Understanding the Purpose for Your Garden" from Chapter 2 to determine what basic goals you want to accomplish. Next, fill all of the aspects of your needs. If you intend to use the space actively for entertaining, how many people and how often will this occur? Be sure to allow for each intended activity. What will be the purpose for entertaining, social or business? Will your intention be to attract new clients? If so, you may try to locate the entertaining space in the Helpful People, Wealth, or Fame area of the Ba-Gua. If it is for your friends and to strengthen relationships, maybe there is space in the Relationship area.

Step 3. Now is the time to walk around your property. Using an overlay on your assessment sheet, note any areas that are sloping or uncomfortable land forms. In the next chapter we will look again at exterior factors that could affect your land and may need a "fix" through a feng shui adjustment. Also note large trees.

Look for anything that you can see that is impinging on your space. For instance, look for buildings that tower over your space.

Search for any great views you can "borrow" into your landscape such as trees, mountains, lakes, or rivers.

Look specifically for areas that may be too dark (yin) or too bright and hot (yang) and record those.

Note any sections that have too many other yin or yang elements such as overgrown leafy plants (yin) or wall to wall pavement (yang).

Think about how you could adjust them such as trimming overgrown areas or adding container planting or a water garden to paved areas.

Observe the five elements at work in the garden. If you are adjacent to a forest, you may want to make adjustments for the excess of that element. If you have picket fences around the property, you may want to add more water element. Conversely, if there is an absence of flat ground or water elements, you will want to consider adding those elements to attain the balance for the land.

If you have any feelings that come up during your walk around, note those as well. For instance, if there is a place in your garden that you just don't like, think about how you can balance or change it. Conversely, if there are areas that you just love, think about how that feeling can be expanded to other areas. Sometimes bringing a plant throughout the garden maintains the good feeling captured in one area.

Step 4. The last step is assessing your emotional needs for the garden.

Begin by thinking about gardens that you remember with fondness. Memories of special gardens can be from childhood, traveling, or the neighborhood. Other sources are magazines or books that you love. Many of my clients clip pictures from magazines to give me ideas of the look or feel they would like in their gardens. These examples can be very helpful because what one person views as a mess is another person's English garden.

Dreaming Your Garden

Many people need a framework for imagining the garden or garden elements. What would they love to include in their landscape? Here is a simple exercise that can help. Read through the instructions and then enjoy the process.

Close your eyes and relax. Take three deep slow breaths to help ease your mind. Imagine sitting and watching a leaf blow in front of you. It is blowing in the wind and when a gust takes it upward, let your imagination follow it up into the sky. Now it is traveling through a cool thick cloudbank. As you and the leaf emerge from the clouds you see below a beautiful garden. Let your thoughts take you down to the ground. This is the most beautiful garden you have ever seen. Spend some time exploring it, remembering to note the colors, fragrances, textures, sounds, and any particular plants that you love here. You can spend as much time as you want. When you are done, imagine the leaf blowing by and your thoughts following it back up into the sky. Before you reenter the cloudbank, turn around and see the garden bathed in a pink, golden light. Return through the clouds and back to your present spot. Know that you can return to this garden or find another image any time you wish.

 Besides accessing your fond memories of gardens, it is important engage the five senses. To experience new potential additions to your garden, you may want to go to a local botanical garden, nursery, or garden tour.

Search for the plants that appeal to your senses and emotions. Look for the colors that you love. Smell your way through the nursery to see which plants carry your favorite fragrances. Notice which textures appeal to your eye and your touch. Ask which plants attract birds or bees and rustle grass-like plants or bamboo to see how you feel about those. Find the herbs or vegetables that you may want to include. Keep notes on the names of the plants and the things you love about them.

Now finish reading this chapter to find the plants and elements to include in each area of the Ba-Gua. The lists in this chapter are just a starting point. The plant world is so rich, many books are just on plants of one color. You can either use one of the suggested plants or do your own research for alternatives. Be sure that the plants listed will thrive in your location and are available through local nurseries or catalogues.

The Fu Dogs of Plants

Fu Dogs are considered to be sacred guardians originally of Buddhist temples and later were also used for personal residences. These guard against evil spirits and evil doers but also are considered to foster happiness and promote prosperity.

In China, Mugwort (Artemisia vulgaris) is hung over the door around the time of the Dragon Festival to keep the evil demons away. In Russia, the Birch Tree (Betula alba) is planted as protection against the evil eye. In North Europe, the Elder Tree (Sambucus nigra) was supposed to ward off evil influence and give protection from witches. Foxglove (Digitalis purpurea) is said to protect against ghosts, evil, and sorcery. There are many other plants that can be used around the entrance to the property or the house for protection from evil spirits. These plants are drawn from a number of cultures and include

Common Name	**Botanical Name**	**How It Works**
Acacia	Acacia spp	keeps demons and ghosts away,
Agrimony	Agrimonia eupatoria	purifies and protects from witchcraft
Ague Root	Aletris farcinosa	wards off evil and protects the house

Common Name	**Botanical Name**	**How It Works**
Aloe	Aloe vera	protects home from negativity
Ash	Fraxinus spp	protect you and all who enter
Avens	Geum urbanum	wards off spirits & venomous beasts,
Basil		is the protecting spirit of the family
Bay Laurel	Lauris nobilis	protects from disasters
Betony	Stachys Betonica	drives away devils and despair
Cedar	Cedrus spp.	purifies and protects your property
Cypress	Cupressus sempervirens	protects your property
Dogwoods	Pyiscidia erythrina	deters evil influences
Dragon's Blood	Draceana drago	is a fabulously protective dragon
Elm	Ulmus spp.	protect property & attract good luck
Fennel	Foeniculum vulgare	prevent witchcraft & evil influences
Ferns	Pteris aquiline	protects everything in the house
Foxglove	Digitalis purpurea	prevents evil & from entering
Garlic	Allium sativum	protects from evil creatures,
Geranium	Pelargonium maculatum	protects from evil, unwanted visitors
Hawthorn	Crataegus oxyacantha	protects from evil influences
Hazel	Corylus aveliana	protects homes especially from fire
Holly	Ilex aquifolium	protects you against lightning
Juniper	Juniperus spp.	guards from accidents, enemies, evil,
Lavender	Lavendula angustifolia	repels negativity from your home
Lilac	Syringia vulgaris	repels evil where planted or strewn
Marigold	Calendula officinalis	protects and attracts positive energy
Marjoram	Organum marjorana	protects your home inside and out
Mullein	Verbascum Thapsus	wards off curses and evil spirits
Oleander	Nerium oleander	protects especially at property edge
Orange Tree	Citrus auranthium	protects and brings good luck
Peach	Prunus persica	protects from evil influences

Common Name	**Botanical Name**	**How It Works**
Pennyroyal	Mentha pulegium	protects your home, repels negativity
Peony	Paeonia officinalis	banishes negative spirits from home
Pepper	Piper nigrum	repels negativity, protects your home
Pine	Pinus spp.	purifies, fosters immortality, fertility
Rosemary	Rosmarinus officinalis	protects your home against thieves
Rowan	Pyrus aucuparia	protects against malevolent beings
Snapdragon	Antirrhinum magus	dispels negativity, increases positive
Solomons Seal	Polygonatum multiflorum	protects the occupants
Strawberry Tree	Arbutus unedo	dispels witches, protects ill children
Sunflower	Helianthus annus	brings safety and protection
Ti	Cordyline fruitcosa	repels negativity, blesses your home
Turmeric	Curcuma longa	protects especially at the front door
Vervain	Verbena officinalis	protects against vampires, evil spirits
Wormwood	Artemisia absinthium	protects as a shield for your property.

Examining Each Gua

Contemplating plants is a favorite pastime for plant lovers. This section will delight you with the variety of plants and elements that will be examined. Each Gua has a chart for the suggested plants, using the color of the Gua as the basis and divided in categories of trees, shrubs, perennials and vines. The chart lists plants that are hardy in various areas of the country and the world. Check with local sources to determine which plants can grow in your area. A discussion section in each Gua following the chart includes information about plants used because of special characteristics or associations which are appropriate for the Gua. Legends, stories, and attributes grow up around plants that have healing or spiritual qualities associated with them. The stories, legends, or healing qualities of plants are important to help us make an emotional connection to them and develop a personal relationship with them. Any particular plant that appeals to you either emotionally or because you wish to have the healing quality of that plant in your garden should be used. Included in the discussion are other decorative items that are useful for a particular area. In the Guas that also have one of the five elements, plants and other suggestions are offered to represent an aspect of the five elements. Only the Guas with elements have a discussion of seasons and senses since only the elements have those associations.

The Benefactors or Helpful People Gua

Beginning in the front of the property, the Benefactors or Helpful People area of the Ba-Gua is represented by the color gray. The gray foliage plants provide a nice contrast in the garden and many gray plants have the added bonus of being drought tolerant. This area is named Ch'ien which translates as "heaven" so we can integrate symbols that are associated with this. Besides Helpful People or Benefactors, this Gua represents travel and the father and males of the household and the head part of the body.

Gray Colored Plants

Trees	Shrubs	Perennials
Eucalyptus;	*Sargent Juniper*	*Dusty miller*
e.g., Silver Dollar Gum	*Blue Chip Juniper*	*Lamb's Ears*
White Ironbark	*Blue Carpet Juniper*	*Dwarf Blue Fescue*
Big Fruited Gum	*Silverberry*	*Tanacetum*
Ghost Gum	*Everlasting*	*Silver King*
Atlas Cedar	*Pussy Willows*	*Mugwort*
Olive	*Bush Germander*	*Mendecino Reed Grass*
Acacia	*Agave*	*Sheep's Fescue*
Cedar of Lebanon	*Russian Olive*	
Silver Linden	*Honey Bush*	**Vines**
Alligator Juniper	*Russian Sage*	*Silver Morning Glory*

Silver Mountain Gum's fragrant branches are used in flower arrangements and hummingbirds love to nest in it. A small-scale tree that is one of my favorites because of its yummy fruit is the *Pineapple Guava*. Its beautiful red flowers are also edible and a striking addition to salads. *Cedrela* is linked in Chinese culture to the father of a family and is used medicinally for bruises, lungs, and earaches. Its wood was considered sacred by the Maya, who carved images on it. *Red Cedar's* bark is used as a mourning staff for fathers and is planted for its edible young shoots. A sacred grove of Cedars leads to the tomb of Confucius. The trunks are old and knotted, which make a path worthy of contemplation, and represent fortitude, grandeur, and incorruptible virtue. Cedar can also be used in the Center area, as it is a symbol of longevity.

Trees that can be used in this area for their association with the father of the family are the Pine and the Oak. *Pines* are essential to the garden because they don't wither in the winter and therefore stand for friends that hold fast in the time of adversity and virtue. They symbolize age, silence, and solitude. They were used in gravesites because it was believed that their vital force will keep the body from decay and strengthen the spirit of the departed. They are often paired with the crane as a motif for longevity and so can also be used in the Center area. *Oaks* are the symbol of masculine strength. Its various parts are used medicinally as an antimicrobial agent in colds, flu, urinary and viral infections, in making inks and dyes, and in tanning.

The support, strength and flexibility of the *Bamboo* is a good quality to have in the Benefactor's area. The *Bush Morning Glory* is a wonderful gray shrub that actually shines silver in the sun. *Lavender Cotton* is a plant that is often used as edging (looks great around a rose garden) and is used as a moth repellent in drawers. A shrub often used in bridal bouquets is *Blue Mist*.

Many of our familiar herbs that have medicinal qualities are gray foliaged plants. *Lavender, Thyme, Mullein,* and *Sage* will provide smells, tastes and, sights that are delightful. Lavender is an emblem of tranquility and purity, which makes it appropriate to use in the Children's Gua also. Lavender's name comes from the Latin word *lavare* which means "to wash" because it was spread under the bedding after washing to infuse the fragrance. This fits perfectly with our understanding of its ability to relax and soothe us as well as its properties as an antibacterial and antifungal agent. *Thyme* stands for courage and has been brewed as a tea with other herbs to help one connect with the

Lavender is a sweet smelling enhancement to Ch'ien.

deva spirits. *Mullein* is another herb that inspires courage and is used to protect from evil attacks and wild animals. *Sage,* which means "to save or be in good health," has long been prized for its powers of longevity. It can be used in the center and in the Wealth Guas for its association with longevity and prosperity. Another herb that is a must in the feng shui garden is *Yarrow*. Yarrow sticks were used in the original method of divination to consult *I Ching*. Many varieties of Yarrow are gray foliage and the flowers are a range of reds, pinks, yellows, and white.

Besides color we can also look at symbolism to enhance areas. As this is the "heaven" Gua, we can add plants to this area that support or foster our path to enlightenment. *Viburnum* is known as the "embroidered ball" or "flower of the Eight Immortals of Taoism." These immortals are like our Western saints and are said to guard the home and bring the owners everything that is valued in life. *Orchids* are admired as a prototype of a perfect personality because their fragrance is not overwhelming. They represent nobility and culture. It was said that one whiff is enough to bestow enlightenment. They are prized for their uprightness, and their delicacy relates a spiritual quality. The *Lotus*, symbolic of perfection, purity and integrity, holds a special place in Buddhist symbolism as an emblem of humans who struggle through the slime of the material world to find enlightenment. It also is considered exceptional because all parts of it are useful. The tubers are eaten and often given to sick people, the fruit is eaten, and the leaves are used to wrap things. This can also be used in the Children's area because of its association with purity or the Knowledge area for its association with spiritual development.

Certain shapes of trees can be used in various sections to attract good energy to that area. In the Ch'ien Gua, a vase-shaped tree such as the *Shamel Ash, Purple Flowering Plum Tree* or *Bloodgood Red Maple* will help to funnel good luck and benefactors into your life.

Other Elements to Enhance the Benefactors Area

Because rocks can be symbolic of heaven and spirituality, they are good for this Gua and lend interest and depth to the garden. When designing the rocks for this area I suggest that you use mountain-like rocks to enhance this area. I always try to select rocks that are similar to the indigenous rocks around your home. If there are mountains around the property, this is an ideal Gua to "borrow the view" of them.

Heaven-shaped rock

You could place a labyrinth or mandala or other shapes that encourage contemplation in this Gua. To enjoy it, you could add a bench or swing in this area.

Improving the Benefactors can bring new clients to you if you own your own business or sellers to you if you are selling your house. When my clients are selling their homes or looking for helpers, I suggest they add a light in this corner. If possible, it should shine upwards to lift the energy here. Another good alternative is a wind chime in this area.

The Career Gua

The representative color for the K'an, Career area of the Ba-Gua is black and the part of the body represented is the ears. Black is not a common color found in flowers or leaves but there are many plants that do have black or nearly black berries. Berries often attract birds that add positive energy to the property. This Gua is also represented by the element of water, the season of winter, and the sense of hearing.

Black Plants

Trees	Shrubs	Perrenials
Shadblow	*India Hawthorn*	*Blackberry Lily*
Dogwoods	*Red Flowering Currant*	*Black Calla Lily*
Yew Tree	*Warty Barberry*	*Actaea 'Hillside Black Beauty'*
Monterrey Cypress	*Japanese Aralia*	*Geranium 'Espresso'*
Sour Gum	*St. John's Wort*	
Chinese Fringe Tree	*Evergreen Huckleberry*	**Vines**
Japan Pepper Tree	*Black Haw*	*Passion Fruit*
Chinese Angelica	*English Laurel*	*Black Raspberry*
Luma Tree	*Privet*	*Ivy*
Nannyberry	*Pernettya*	

The *American Elderberry* provides blue-black berries that attract birds, are good in jams and wine, and are said to lower cholesterol, boost the immune system, help coughs, and support heart health. A tree that provides striking black bark in the winter when wet, as well as black berries, is the *Camphor Tree*. It is a natural insect repellent and preservative and is used medicinally to ease inflammation. Other black trunk or branched choices are *Tamarix* and *Japanese Tree Lilac*. The *Black Mission Fig* provides delicious fruit which helps ripen your career hopes. As *Persimmon Trees* represent luck in business, this is a great tree to use in Career.

A tender plant that delights everyone is the *Mickey Mouse Plant*. It has yellow flowers in the spring and black and red berries that develop simultaneously and looks like that famous mouse that gives this plant its name. One of my favorite berried plants is the *True Myrtle*. It is a fragrant evergreen known as a love herb, often used in bridal bouquets, in cooking, and medicinally as an antiseptic. Myrtle because of its association with the feminine can also be used in the Relationship area.

Because this Gua holds the element of water, we can use the different associations with that element in this area. One aspect of the water element is that it represents our hearing sense so plants that encourage the sound of birds

Mickey Mouse plant

66

and bees can be used to enhance this area. Plants that provide food for birds such as *Elderberry, Fig Trees, Oaks, Cotoneasters* and *Firethorns* will ensure their presence. Some common plants that attract hummingbirds include *Toyon, Silk Tree, Butterfly Weed, Columbine, Gladiolus,* and *Bee Balm.*

The water element in a person's ch'i holds the attributes of wisdom, insight, motivation, and social contacts. Plants and elements can be used in this Gua to strengthen these personality aspects. A plant combination used to enrich Chinese gardens and known to symbolize sincere friendship is known as the "four virtuous gentlemen." This is the aggregate of *Plum Tree, Orchids, Bamboo,* and *Chrysanthemum.* The qualities that link them are grace, resilience, nobility, and endurance, the essential ingredients for the ideal gentlemen. The *Plum Tree* also symbolizes winter, the season for water.

A plant that stands for wisdom is the *Cinquefoil*, a creeping groundcover used medicinally as a gargle for sore throats and as an astringent lotion. The *English Hawthorn* benefits all heart conditions and has many legends to support it as a plant for wisdom, fertility, and protection.

Other plants that are associated with the element of water are *Apple, Ash, Burdock, Chamomile, Catnip, Cyclamen, Geranium, Heather, Henbane, Hyacinth, Lovage, Meadowsweet, Myrrh, Orris, Pansy, Periwinkle, Poppy, Violet, and Yarrow.*

The shape of tree best used in this area is a triangular or pyramidal shaped tree. Trees such as *American Linden, White Fir, Sweet Gum Tree, Bald Cypress* and *Pin Oak* will fit the bill. These trees lift your career in a positive direction.

Other Elements to Enhance the Career Area

Because water is the element of this Gua, if you wish to enhance your career you can use water shapes and elements in this area. This means curving walkways and free-form shapes in the lawn, groundcover, or planting beds.

The actual element of water can be used in the form of a water fountain, pond, or birdbath. Water can also be represented by stones taken from rivers or oceans, fish, turtles, or other water creature motifs that can be used in paving, handrails, and as ornaments along a walkway. Some people use river rock pebbles or shells imbedded in concrete to embellish the look of the pavement. The Chinese used shells for money so integrating them into the paving in the Career area can bring money into your home.

In Chinese culture elephants are a symbol of strength, wisdom, and prudence. Animals can be used in the form of a statue, a symbol in the paving, or as the motif in a flag. The Tortoise is traditionally associated with the water Gua and is considered sacred. The eight trigrams, which are represented in the Ba-Gua, drawn from *I Ching*, are said to have evolved from the markings on the shell of a tortoise. The tortoise stands for longevity, strength, and endurance so it can also be used in the center of the property.

The Knowledge Gua

The color for the Knowledge section of the Ba-Gua is blue. Blue is another unusual color in nature but trees and shrubs exhibit this color through their flowers, foliage, and berries. The most startling blue flowers are seen in the perennial category. The *I Ching* symbol for the Ken area means "mountain."

Blue Plants

Trees	Shrubs	Vines
Wild Lilac	*Rose of Sharon*	*Clematis*
Blue Spruce	*Bluebeard*	*Blueberry*
Tolleson's Blue Juniper	*Sawara False Cypress*	*Sky Flower Vine*
Blue Atlantic Ceder	*Oregon Grape*	*Wisteria*
China Fir ('Glauca')	*Darwin Barberry*	**Perennials**
Douglas Fir ('Glauca')	*Hydrangea (Acid soil)*	*Virginia Bluebells*
Blue Mountain Hemlock	*'Blue Moon' Rose*	*Pincushion*
Harlequin Glorybower	*Germander*	*Blue Star*
Tatarian Dogwood	*Blue Weed*	*False Indigo*
Blue Elderberry	*Russian Sage*	*Blue Flax*
		Blue Lily of the Nile
		Blue Fescue
		Catmint

Banana shrub

The *Chaste Tree* is of Mediterranean derivative and has many medicinal qualities to support female hormonal health. Its name is from its reputation to reduce libido and promote chastity. The beautiful *Blue Hibiscus* is a good choice for a profuse and continuously blooming shrub. One of the great hardy shrubs, ground cover and herbs is *Rosemary,* meaning 'Dew of the Sea." Not only is its flower blue but the foliage is a blue-green. It is as good for slope erosion control as it is in your most flavorful stews. It is also an herb of love so it could also be used in the Relationship Gua. One of my favorite shrubs which flowers blue, purple, pink, and white is the *Butterfly Bush*. It is striking when in flower and attracts-guess what! *Cape Plumbago* is a vine that flowers profusely with clear blue flowers and is great at holding a hill against soil erosion.

In ancient China, the penniless scholar unable to afford paper would use the wide leaves of a *Banana* to write on and so this plant has become the symbol for self-improvement. They are highly valued for the sounds of rain and wind on their leaves and for their delicious fruit.

Peach and *Plum Trees* represent brotherliness, which resembles the teacher/ student relationship, so it may go well in Knowledge.

Camellias were important in the Chinese garden for their beautiful foliage and wonderful winter flowers. The most valued varieties are used in making tea and oils for the hair. Buddhists drank the tea during long meditation sessions that led to spiritual enlightenment. The *Olive Tree* is often used as one of the rewards of literary merit and as a symbol of study. Its petals are used to scent teas. As a symbol of autumn it could also be used in the Children's Gua. The *Chinese Scholar Tree* has always been associated with places of higher learning. The life of a retired scholar is often depicted as a person sitting under a *Palm Tree.* As such, retired scholars often carry palm leaves as an indication of their leisurely status.

Plants in other traditions used to increase intellectual knowledge are *Balm of Gilead, Benzoin, Rosemary,* and *Rue.*

The shape of a tree that is used in this area is the pyramidal shaped tree as in the Career area. It symbolizes that you will advance in your knowledge and wisdom. Trees that are this shape are the *Coast Redwood, Katsura Tree,* and *Turkish Filbert.* The *Katsura Tree* smells like cotton candy or brown sugar in the fall when it loses its leaves.

Other Elements to Enhance the Knowledge Area

Because the Knowledge Gua is emblematic of spiritual wisdom as well as intellectual knowledge, this is a good spot to locate a meditation space if feasible. The cool blue colors of this Gua are conducive to the practice of contemplation. A focus for meditative practice could be an object such as a blue gazing ball or religious emblem of your own choosing.

While the primary area to place mountain-like rocks would be in the Benefactor Gua, because of the *I Ching* meaning of this area, adding rocks in this area would also be appropriate.

The Family Gua

The color green represents the family or ancestor area, Chen. Of course, most plants are green but the plants used to represent this area will generally be non-flowering plants with insignificant or green flowers or green-barked plants. The name from the *I Ching* for this area means "thunder." This is where the element of wood is found and it represents the season of spring and the sense of sight.

Green Plants

Trees	Shrubs	Vines
Australian Willow	*Fern*	*Creeping Fig Vine*
Pine e.g. White Pine	*Boxwood*	*Boston Ivy*
Indian Laurel Tree	*Tobira*	
English Yew	*Aucuba*	**Perennials**
Maple Tree	*False Aralia*	*Hosta*
European Beech	*Evergreen Euonymus*	*Dinosaur Food*
Lombardy Poplar	*Hopseed Bush*	*Baby's Tears*
Cucumber Tree	*Toyon Staghorn Sumac*	*Irish Moss*
Little Leafed Linden	*Xylosma*	
Oak Tree		

The *Pine Tree* represents longevity and this is a good quality to have for our elders. The *Sweet Bay* is known as the tree that celebrates poets and athletes (think of the Olympic crown) and is used to flavor spaghetti and stews. Its aromatic leaves have antioxidant and anti-inflammatory healing powers. The beautiful, slow-growing *Bo Tree* is the tree Buddha sat under when he gained enlightenment so this beauty can be used here or in the Knowledge Gua. The *Black Pine* is a conifer traditionally used in Japanese Zen gardens and Bonsai.

The *Bamboo* family is a group of giant grasses that sound delightful blowing in the wind. It is important to inform yourself about the attributes of Bamboo because while running varieties are rampant invasive growers, the clumping varieties will be well mannered in your garden.

English Ivy, a member of the Ginseng family, is used medicinally for cuts, sores, and skin problems. The *Common Hop Vine* produces the flavor for beer. The light green hops have a fresh, piney fragrance and can be cooked as a vegetable or used medicinally as a sedative.

The *Tree Peony* in Chinese culture represents spring of the year, an aspect of the wood element. If you can't resist using colors in this area, choose spring bulbs or plants that flower in the spring such as *Geraniums, Coral Bells, Primrose, Clematis, Azaleas, Camellias, Beauty Bush, Flowering Quince, Dogwood, Flowering Plums, Pears,* and *Horsechestnut.*

Black Bamboo is invasive.

The attributes of wood in a person's ch'i are steadfastness and benevolence. There are many plants to support these qualities. The *Dogwood,* whose spring bloom signaled Indians that it was time to plant corn, is used medicinally to break fevers and relieve sore muscles. The *Oak* is a sacred tree in many cultures, revered for its strength and endurance. *Vervain* was called by the Chinese "Dragon's teeth grass" and "iron vervain," which suggest hidden powers. *Bamboo, Pine,* and *Elderberry* are also symbols of a steadfast nature. All parts of the *Sunflower,* cultivated by American Indians over 3,000 years ago, are useful. *Basil* promotes compassion between two people. It is used in church holy water because it was found growing around Christ's tomb after the resurrection. *Sweet Marjoram* is said to have been created by Aphrodite as a symbol of happiness.

The element wood represents the sense of sight and the season of spring. Enhancing sight could mean contrasting the textures of plants and elements used here. Using bold and fine textures will lend interest to the area; for instance a *Dinosaur Food* (bold) among the *Yew* or *Pine* (fine) will provide a dramatic contrast. Kuan Yin, the Chinese Goddess of Mercy, holds a willow branch in her hand as a source of protection and blessing. Willows, a symbol of spring, are used for making baskets, ropes, and healing herbs. They were thought to be supernatural protection from invaders.

The shape of a tree that is used in this area is the round-headed tree such as *Italian Stone Pine, Flowering Crabapple, Black Locust, and Ohio Buckeye.* The round-headed tree brings completeness and harmony to your family.

Other Elements to Enhance the Family Area

The other elements that are used in this Gua would be anything related to ancestors and family or the element wood. This is a good location for the garden swing that has been in the family for generations. Tall, narrow-shaped elements are used to represent wood. Columns, narrow structures, and columnar shaped plants are examples of the wood shape. This would be a good area to add an overhead structure with substantial posts. If this area is a side yard, add a hedge using columnar plants such as *Italian Cypress.* If the area is a courtyard or a paved space, using decorative columns to hold pots and to lend height and interest to this wood area.

If walls are used here, perhaps they are painted green. Wood fences may emphasize the vertical shape, such as using bamboo pickets which exhibit a repeating wood shape.

Traditional Chinese pagodas could be located in the Family area as historically they were used to hold ancient, sacred, or ancestral relics. They could also be located in the Benefactor's area or in the Knowledge area. Pagodas carry beneficent influences and were often built to exercise a good influence or luck in an area or to chase away the negative energy of an area. Some people believe that the pagoda is a representative of the mountain and so brings the heavenly influence to an area. In the event a full-size pagoda is not appropriate here, a pagoda lantern may be used.

In the Family area of my property I placed a beautiful wood art piece that has a lotus, symbol of enlightenment, as its centerpiece. It represents my hope for peace and better lifetimes for my ancestors.

The Wealth Gua

The primary color for the Wealth area is purple. I wonder whether I love this area because it represents wealth, abundance, and good fortune or because I love purple. It is difficult to restrain the selections here because nature provides us with such a plethora of gorgeous and luscious purple plants.

Purple Plants

Trees	Shrubs	Vines
Jacaranda	*Pride of Madera*	*Violet Trumpet Vine*
Texas Mountain Laurel	*Bush Mexican Sage*	*Lavender Starflower*
Crepe Myrtle	*Paraguay Nightshade*	*Lilac Vine*
Japanese Lilac Tree	*Mountain Laurel*	*Trailing Lantana*
Empress Tree	*Chaste Tree*	*Royal Trumpet Vine*
Saucer Magnolia	*Beautyberry*	**Perennials**
Purple Orchid Tree	*Southern Heath*	*Sea Lavender*
Lilac Melaleuca	*Scotch Heather*	*Monkshood*
Desert Willow	*Showy Hebe*	*Liatris*
Oklahoma Redbud	*Fuschia*	*Periwinkle*
Desert Willow	*Carpet Bugle*	

Princess flower has eye-popping purple flowers.

The *Princess Flower* is a small-scale tree that not only blooms a striking royal purple color but its leaves have a reddish tinge that are soft to touch. One of the most beloved plants used for perfumes is the *Lilac Tree*. It is used medicinally to reduce fever, expel intestinal worms, and prevent the recurrence of symptoms of disease like malaria. The *Yesterday, Today and Tomorrow* plant is engaging because its impressive purple fragrant flowers fade to a soft lavender and then to white.

The *Purple Cornflower* has gained notoriety and favor recently as the immune system support, Echinacea.

The *Tree Peony*, called King of Flowers in China, is the embodiment of aristocracy, leisure, wealth, rank, and beautiful women. Its flowers are spectacular and the bark is good for blood disorders. The *Catalpa*, a symbol of good luck, is used as the wood for imperial coffins. The changing of its leaves signaled the autumn festival so it could also be used in the Children's area.

There are many plants used through various cultures to increase prosperity and good luck. *Cedar Trees* bestow prosperity as well as treat rheumatic afflictions. In China, they are known as "Trees of Faithful Love" and so will also enhance the relationship Gua. *Elder Trees* are also used medicinally for skin ailments and colds. *Basil* is also useful in flavoring foods and as a tea to aid digestion. *Chamomile*, a useful groundcover, is used as a relaxing tea and in a bath relieves sunburn. *Cinnamon* is useful as a spice but also good for colds and digestive problems. *Jasmine* and *Honeysuckle* are primarily used for perfume and aromatherapy. *Mint* is good for indigestion, colds, and in pain-relieving balms but watch out for this rampant spreader. *Sage* is known for its contributions to longevity as well as prosperity. It aids digestion and is antiseptic and antifungal. *Poppies* are the source for morphine and codeine and its seeds are delicious in cakes. If the *Narcissus*, known as Fairy Lily, blooms at the time of Chinese New Year it indicates good fortune for the year. An *Orange* tree is thought to bring abundant happiness and prosperity. *Orange* peel is used as a diuretic and for improving digestive properties. As a matter of fact, all citruses, especially *Kumquat* are thought to enhance prosperity. Kumquats are thought of as gold and given out at Chinese New Year as a wish to others for a prosperous year. Other plants used for Wealth are *Tiger Lily, Grape, Nigella, Oak, Wheat, White Clover, Lavender, Red Rose, and Shamrock.*

In the Wealth area, the round-headed tree is the shape to use so that you will have more money. Trees such as *White Ash, Plains Cottonwood, Sugar Maple,* and *Red Oak* will help with your abundance and good luck. Round-headed trees symbolize that you will receive the fruit of your hard work so the purple *Jacaranda* would be perfect here as well as the *Strawberry Tree,* which produces red fruit.

Other Elements to Enhance the Wealth Area

Fish are the perennial Chinese symbol of wealth and abundance. They are also emblems of harmony and freedom. Monkeys are believed to bestow success by keeping away the malicious spirits that prevent success. The Rat is a symbol of industry and prosperity for its ability for locating, acquiring, and hoarding abundant food supplies. (Our other associations with this creature make it a less desirable symbol for our gardens.) Dogs are a symbol of future prosperity. Frogs are used to symbolize auspiciousness and money. Whales are a symbol of wealth and abundance. Any of these emblems can be used as statues or motifs in the Wealth area to attract more prosperity.

Moving water will activate any area but in the Wealth area it is particularly good. The best way to express this moving water is jetting it up in the air as opposed to falling water. Regardless of whether it jets up or falls down, it is best if it is directed toward your house. When I first designed my current garden, there was a Jacuzzi in my Wealth corner with a white lattice fence around the space. I was thinking small at first and installed purple-colored flags in this area to enhance my wealth. A visiting colleague suggested that I add more color to the space. The next week my lattice was painted purple and my income increased by threefold immediately.

It is better to avoid a fireplace or barbecue in the very corner of the Wealth corner because it can burn up your money. If you already have one in this area, you can add plants; specifically, nine potted plants around it adjust for this element.

In addition to using plants, elements, and symbols to enhance this area, one of the most powerful tools to increase the energy in any area is your imagination. If you consider the energy embodied in an area and capture the spirit of that energy, you will create a personally powerful area for yourself. For instance, in this Gua the space would capture luxury and abundance. Some people think of luxury in terms of costly looking items such as imported pots. Others see it as a means to freedom and leisure and may wish to use hammocks and lawn furniture here. Whatever the image used, it should be created with style and flourish.

The Fame Gua

Vibrant red is the representative color for the Fame area. It is a color that is easily found in flowering red plants, red berries which attract birds and bees, and red fall foliage plants. This is also the area of the element of Fire, the season of summer, and the sense of taste.

Red Plants

Trees	Shrubs	Vines
Red Flowering Gum	*Tropical Hibiscus*	*Blood Red Trumpet Vine*
Hawthorn	*Poinsettia*	*Common Trumpet Creeper*
Crabapple	*Canna*	*Cape Honeysuckle*
African Tulip Tree	*Firethorn*	**Perennials**
New Zealand Christmas Tree	*Camellia*	*Cardinal Flower*
Mountain Ash	*Holly*	*Penstemon*
Red Oak	*Weigelia*	*Red Valerian*
Smoke Tree	*Flowering Quince*	*Hollyhocks*
Sweet Gum Tree	*Cranberry Cotoneaster*	*False Spirea*
Red Horsechestnut	*Skimmia*	*Maltese Cross*
Firewheel Tree	*Red Hot Poker*	

Among the trees that are most spectacular are the *Coral Trees,* which display unique, beautiful red flowers and have outstanding structural shape. I compete with the birds for the red delicious winter berries on the *Strawberry Tree*. A tree that gives us syrup, candy, and brilliant red fall color is the *Maple Tree.*

The *Bottlebrush* produces red flowers that attract hummingbirds. *Heavenly Bamboo,* which produces red berries and reddish new foliage, is not a true bamboo. It has a beautiful texture and is successfully grown in pots or used as bonsai.

In tropical regions one of the most beloved and showiest red flowering vines is the *Bougainvillea. Red Spike Ice Plant* is a drought-tolerant ground cover. Many of the *Red Sage* plants have wonderful fragrances such as the *Pineapple Sage* that can be used to flavor teas.

The sense of taste may be represented by a vegetable garden located here including varieties of tomatoes or red peppers, watermelon, beets, and radishes. Herbs including *Amaranth* and *Bee Balm* could be included for their red flowers. The phoenix, is the animal associated with fire so the *Chinese Parasol Tree* (Firmania simplex), thought to be the perch for the Chinese phoenix would be appropriately located here. This tree has edible seeds eaten in moon cakes at the Chinese autumn festival. Because it marks the progress of autumn by losing one leaf a day, it is also appropriate in the Children's area that represents the autumn season. It is also associated with scholars and so can be planted in the Knowledge area. *Azaleas* have been allied with blood and fire and its roots are used in making furniture. *Lotus*, the plant symbol of summer, could also be placed here.

The aspects of a person's ch'i represented by the fire Gua are reason, expressiveness, and etiquette. There are many plants that support the fire aspects of a person's nature. *Angelica* blooms around the feast day of the Archangel Michael, who is said to have appeared to explain its protective powers. It is used medicinally for colds and aromatically in potpourri. The *Carnation*, symbolizing admiration, was a flower of the divinity to the Greeks and is used medicinally as a nerve tonic in wine. *Garlic*, my favorite spice, is known as a blood cleanser, as a deterrent for colds, and as an effective agent in reducing cholesterol. Both Michelangelo and Leonardo da Vinci used *Rue* to improve their eyesight and creative forces. Its leaves are used to bathe tired eyes. It is also said to have inspired the design of the club suit in playing cards. Other plants that represent the reason, expressiveness, and etiquette are: *Alder, Basil, Bay Laurel, Betony, Cinnamon, Clove, Heliotrope, Holly, Juniper, Marigold, Mullein, Oak, Pennyroyal, Pepper, Primrose, Rosemary, Saffron, St John's Wort, Vanilla,* and *Vervain.*

Kangaroo paws have both spiky leaves and red flowers.

The shape of tree in this area could be a columnar tree which can help you to advance in promotion and fame. Typical of this shape would be the *Italian Cypress,* which is considered to be stately. One of my personal favorites in this area is the *Hollywood Juniper*. Its shape isn't exactly columnar but it very closely resembles flames. Other trees that are shaped for this area are *Lombardy Poplar, European Hornbeam, Tulip Tree,* and *the European Aspen.*

Hollywood Juniper

Other Elements for the Fame Area

Pointed shapes, the sense of taste, and the summer season represent the fire element. In the other areas of the Gua pointed plants and elements are avoided because of the danger of secret arrows. In the fire Gua, although they must be carefully placed to avoid barbs pointing at the house, spiky plants and elements are encouraged. This means a pointed or radiating trellis, a pointed roofed gazebo, a wood picket fence, or a bold plant such as *New Zealand Flax* may be used here.

This is the area of excitement and lively interaction so plan a fire pit, barbecue, pizza oven, or fireplace to enjoy with friends and relatives. Don't forget special lighting here too in the form of sconces or candles.

In Chinese culture, animals are one of the representatives of fire so your favorite deer topiary would fit nicely in this Gua.

The Fame area represents what the world thinks of you. Here you may wish to create something that symbolizes the image you want the world to see or something that shows how you earn your reputation. One of my clients represents mural artists and has a wall mural painted in her Fame area. I have a sun sculpture in my Fame area which has helped my reputation from the day I placed it. You can also use the fire element to express flair or flamboyance.

The Marriage or Relationship Gua

The Marriage or Relationship area, K'un, known as "earth", is represented by the color pink. The energy carried in this Gua is one of mother, the most feminine and nurturing of energies. This area represents all types of partnerships, especially our love relationships but also business partnerships. Nature provides us with a plethora of pink flowering species.

Peonies

Pink Plants

Trees	**Shrubs**	**Vine**
Cape Chestnut	*Rockrose*	*Pink Trumpet Vine*
Flowering Cherry	*Oleander*	*Mandevilla*
Ch'i talpa	*Glossy Abelia*	*Sweet Pea Vine*
Idaho Locust	*Pink Escallonia*	**Perennials**
Flowering Plum	*Beauty Bush*	*Sweet Rocket*
Tamarisk	*Mountain Laurel*	*Bergenia*
Pink Trumpet Tree	*Azaleas*	*London Pride*
Flowering Almond	*Redvein Enkianthus*	*Creeping Thyme*
Chinese Cedrela	*Geraldton Waxflower*	*Meadowrue*
Primrose Tree	*Tree Mallow*	*Phlox*

The breath taking *Floss Silk Tree* blooms profusely from fall to winter and displays white balls resembling spectacular cotton balls following the flowers. The *Silk Tree,* also known as the *Mimosa,* has fluffy pink flowers in the summer and is known to Native Americans as a teacher about our feminine nature and loving heart.

Pink Breath of Heaven in flower is absolutely true to its name. The most appropriate shrub in the Relationship area is the *Rose*. There are people who question Roses in the Marriage area because of its thorns but the thorns are indicative of the nature of relationships: sweet with prickly aspects. Not only can rose petals be used in salads and pies and to make syrups, wine, and teas, but it also can purify the environment and symbolize love.

Iceplant that blooms all spring and summer makes a spectacular show of hilly areas as well as protecting homes from fire disasters. Other perennials that are enjoyable in the garden are: *Thrift* which attracts butterflies, *Bleeding Hearts* for the liberal gardener, and *Obedient Plant* for old fashioned thinkers. *Obedient Plant* is a playful plant for children because when bent it will remain in position.

There are many symbols of feminine grace, mother, and good relationships in the Chinese culture. Though *Willow* is symbolic of feminine grace, they should never be planted in the back-yard because the shape and Chinese name signify that the husband or wife will end up sad. Kuan Yin, the Chinese Goddess of Mercy who is a particular protector of women and children, is a good symbol to add to this area. A very important *Mulberry Tree* is the symbol of the day, the comforts of home, and human activity. Its wood is used to make a mourning staff for a Chinese mother and it is essential to the silk-making industry. *Apricots, Azaleas, Cherry,* and *Apple* blossoms are considered to be emblems of feminine beauty. The fruit of an apple is a symbol of friendship and protection. *Day Lilies* are symbolic of the mother of the family. *Jasmine*, used in Greek times as a charm against sorcery, is used by the Chinese to scent teas and make perfumes. The flower is an emblem of women and a symbol of sweetness. The *Magnolia Tree* represents feminine sweetness and beauty.

Relationships and marriage are among the most prevalent concerns of people; consequently, lucky symbols have developed all over the world. *Rosemary,* with its reputation for strengthening the memory, has become an emblem of fidelity for lovers. It stimulates circulation and eases pain by increasing blood supply. *Balm of Gilead* was said to be a gift from the Queen of Sheba to Solomon. Its musk fragrance is used in men's perfumes and is used in creams to relieve arthritic pain. *Catnip* attracts bees if they can get by the cats that love this plant. It is used in salads and medicines for headaches, upset stomachs, and as a mild sedative. Known by the ancient Egyptians as a soothing herb, *Dill* was used in the middle ages by magicians in their spells and by common folk in wine to enhance passion. Today it is primarily used to spice and pickle foods and to soothe colicky babies. *Gardenias* have always engendered romantic thoughts and are known as the happiness flower for their ability to relieve restlessness and irritability. In China women wear them in their hair and use them in perfumes and to scent tea. *Marjoram*, which grows wild in the Mediterranean hills, is known as "joy of the mountain." It was worn as wreaths in Greek and Roman weddings to symbolize the joyful event. It is used medicinally as a stomach disorder remedy.

No discussion of relationships can be complete without my favorite romantic story about the *Rose*. It is said that Cleopatra seduced Anthony knee deep in rose petals. What an image to carry in the relationship Gua!

Other plants used to increase love relationships are *Basil, Coriander, Cyclamen, Elder,*

Ferns, Geraniums, Hyacinth, Juniper, Lovage, Marigold, Meadowsweet, Mistletoe, Myrtle, Orange, Pansy, Spearmint, Valerian, Vervain, and *Violet.*

The shape tree that is best for the partnership area is a round-headed tree as in the Family and Wealth areas. Round-headed trees such as *American Yellowwood, Green Ash Tree* and *Amur Corktree* support harmony and smooth partnerships.

Other Elements to Enhance the Relationship Area

Anything that has a heart shape would work well in this area. I have seen beautiful bent wood benches, arbors, and gates that have hearts in their design. You can also consider plants with heart-shaped leaves like the *Pansy Redbud,* which also flowers pink, *Heartleaf Bergenia, Coral Trees, Empress Tree* and *Linden Tree.*

Certain animals in the Chinese culture represent mating and marriage. The Duck is a symbol of conjugal fidelity and happiness because it is said that they maintain a lasting attachment after mating. Likewise, a Goose and Swan mate for life and so are indicative of marriage. Of course, if you use them in the garden, two of them would be the best.

The Relationship area is the place to create the context for the type of relationships that you want to attract. If you want to promote the family relationships, a comfortable deck, gazebo, or seating area here can stage the connections. A love relationship may be fostered by an old-fashioned swing flanked by jasmine vines or climbing roses. A gathering place for artists may have seating bordered by original art, music, or a place for performing arts. Your intention can create a loving atmosphere for what you want to foster.

The Children Gua

The Children's area of the Ba-Gua is represented by the color white, the element of metal, the sense of smell, and the season of autumn. White is an exciting color especially because it can be enjoyed both by sunlight and moonlight. There are many white flowering plants and when you are selecting trees, remember that trees like the *Paperbark Tree*, the *Aspen,* and the *Birch* have white bark.

White Plants

Trees	Shrubs	Vines
Bradford Pear	*Bridal Wreath*	*Easter Lily Vine*
Chinese Fringe Tree	*Snow Drop*	*Chinese Gooseberry*
Snowball Tree	*Deutzia*	*Madagascar Jasmine*
American Yellowwood	*Lily of the Valley Shrub*	*Star Jasmine*
Sourwood Tree	*Sweet Cicely*	*Climbing Hydrangea*
Franklin Tree	*Mexican Orange*	**Perennials**
Dove Tree	*Daphne*	*Calla Lily*
Orange Jasmine	*Pearl Bush*	*Santa Barbara Daisy*
Catalpa	*Irish Heath*	*Japanese Anemone*
Snowdrop Tree	*Mock Orange*	*Fairy Wand*

The *Flaxleaf Paperbark Tree* has a white bark that feels like a soft sponge to touch. Its delicate white summer flowers give the effect of snow on its branches. The *Japanese Pagoda Tree*, also known as the *Chinese Scholar Tree,* blooms through the summer and into the fall. The *Evergreen Magnolia*'s huge, fragrant white flowers are especially beloved in the southern United States.

Several of my favorite shrubs, the heavenly scented *Gardenia,* the striking *Bush Anemone,* and the sweet-scented *Myrtle* are white flowering plants. *Japanese Privet* is a spring and summer flowering shrub that makes an excellent hedge. A plant that has insignificant white flowers but produces a powerfully heady scent is the *Night Blooming Jasmine.*

A vine, which seems to bloom perennially, is the voracious growing *Potato Vine*. The *Silver Lace Vine* is often used in flower arrangements

Gardenias smell heavenly.

and bridal bouquets. All of the *Jasmine Vines* are heavenly smelling additions to the garden.

All matters of children, fertility, and autumn belong in this Gua. *Pomegranate* is a sign of fertility, abundance, and children because of the many seeds in the fruit. My daughter had many Pomegranates in the centerpieces at her wedding. Nine months later, I had a beautiful grandson. *Chrysanthemum,* a Chinese symbol of autumn, an attribute of the metal element, could be placed here. It is also a symbol of longevity and so could also be placed in the center section. It makes a delicious mild herbal tea.

The aspect of a person's ch'i that represents the metal element is purity and righteousness. Plants that relate to these qualities will be helpful in developing these parts of your personality. The beautiful *Magnolia*, called the jade orchid, is often used as a focal plant and considered a symbol of purity. The *Lotus* flower will enhance this area, as it is a symbol of purity and truth. Lotus is used medicinally for relaxing, lowering cholesterol, and benefiting your heart and kidney. *Gardenias, White Lilacs, White Rosebuds,* and *Snowflake* are associated with purity. *Lily of the Valley*, another plant associated with purity, is called Our Lady's Tears as it symbolizes the Virgin Mary. It is used in treating heart ailments and is popular in wedding bouquets.

The shape tree that is good for the Children's Gua is triangular, which symbolizes children growing up and doing well in life. The *Fir, Spruce,* and *American Arborvitae* are good examples of the triangular or pyramidal shaped tree.

Other Elements to Enhance the Children's Area

The Children's area is a place of purity, creativity, and play. Anything that can be used to add artistry, novelty, and fun to this area will awaken those aspects in you. If this area is a narrow side yard, sidewalls can be adorned with creative murals, interesting espaliered plants, or original metal art pieces.

The metal shape is a coin or rounded shape. Arbors can be rounded shapes used as gateways to the Children's area. Round-shaped pots, round stepping stones, and rounded light fixtures would all represent metal. Much of the patio furniture available is white or metal or both and suitable for this area.

The sense of smell is found in many of the plants listed for the Children's Gua. One way to decide which plants to use is to visit a nursery and experience the diversity of smells. Another method is to use an aromatherapy or a Bach flower chart. Aromatherapy and Bach flowers delineate the plants that are used to remedy various physical or emotional conditions. The energy of a plant can begin correcting the imbalance in your ch'i that caused the disorder.

Kuan Yin, the Chinese Goddess of Mercy is most often thought of as a protector of children. A statue of this goddess can be located in the Children's area if her image appeals to you. The Dove is considered to be an emblem of filial duty and can be used here or in the center as it is also a symbol of long life. Sheep are also a symbol of filial piety.

Center of the Property

The center of the Ba-Gua is represented by the element of earth, the color of yellow, and the sense of touch and late summer. The shape associated with earth is a flat, rectangular, or square shape. Flowers as well as fall foliage provide the vibrant colors that are associated with this area. The center is the integration point. Issues other than those mentioned in the eight Guas are caught up here. For instance, health and the result of good health, longevity, is handled at the center.

Yellow Plants

Trees	Shrubs	Vines
Acacia	*Flannel Bush*	*Cat's Claw Vine*
Golden Chain Tree	*Senna*	*Caroline Jessamine*
Ilang Ilang Tree	*Japanese Kerria*	*Guinea Gold Vine*
Tulipwood Tree	*Mexican Caesalpinia*	*Black Eyed Susan Vine*
Mexican Palo Verde	*Yellow Jacobinia*	**Perennials**
Golden Trumpet Tree	*Forsythia*	*Rock Rose*
Tipu Tree	*Jerusalem Sage*	*Wavy-leafed Mullein*
Water Gum	*Yellow Mallow*	*Monkey Flower*
Golden Larch	*Fothergilla*	*Coreopsis*
Elm Trees	*Wintersweet*	*Sunflowers*

The *Sweet Shade Tree* is appropriate for narrow and semi-shady locations and adds a sweet smell to the spring and summer air. A tree that provides bright yellow tulip-shaped spring flowers and bright yellow fall foliage is the *Tulip Tree*. Another tree known for its yellow fall foliage is the *Ginkgo* or *Maidenhair Tree*, which is the darling of the health food stores for its "newly" discovered healing properties. Don't plant a female variety of this tree because although you will still enjoy the soft green leaves and the spectacular gold autumn color, the messy stinky fruit will not be a pleasant experience.

The shrub that represents Los Angeles is the yellow and orange *Bird of Paradise,* which is a great cutting flower. The fragrant *Winter Hazel*'s flowers signal the end of winter and has spectacular fall foliage.

Lantana, a vine often used in erosion control, is a favorite of butterflies. The fragrant rampant *Honeysuckle Vine* is a favorite especially in the south and also provides slopes with erosion control measures. A bright long flowering favorite perennial is the *Euryops Daisy.* *Daylilies* and *Primroses* are beloved perennials.

Chinese culture has developed medicines, exercises, and other practices for maintaining healthy bodies and lengthening life. *Pomegranates* are planted for their spectacular flowers, fruits and as auspicious symbols of longevity. The tall *Pines, Cedars* and *Junipers* sculpted by the weather are valued for their age and as a symbol of longevity. *Chrysanthemum*, yeh Ching, means "soul energy of the sun" and was originally cultivated for wine made from their petals. They are used as a toning herb that cools in the hot weather and are said to contribute to longevity. The Chinese once believed that *Coriander* conferred immortality. It has been mentioned in Sanskrit texts, Egyptian papyri, and the Bible. It can be chewed or steeped in water to help digestion or as a sedative. *Bamboos'* pliant strength suggests hardiness, everlasting resilience, and virtue. Bamboo is often used in front of a wall for a yin-yang contrast. *Hibiscus* was thought to be the tree of immortality. The *Gourd* is a charm for longevity and is used to ward off harmful influences. The *Cassia Tree* is not only good for the bright yellow summer flowers but is said to confer immortality to those who eat it. Its leaves and pods are used in many commercial laxatives.

Fruit trees have a special place in Chinese gardens. *Pears* are signs of longevity and good government. The *Flowering Plum*, friend of winter, and beloved for the combination of its gnarled branches and its spring blossoms, symbolizes renewal of the vitality, age, longevity, rebirth, endurance, and dignity. Lao Tsu, the founder of the Taoist sect, is said to have been born under a plum tree. *The Peach* is the symbol of spring, marriage, good health, and immortality. Many Chinese grow it at the front door to bring good fortune and ward off fever and evil spirits. With its other associations it could be located in the Partnership area or the Family area as well.

Including plants that have different textures as well as plants that are interesting to touch can foster the sense of touch. Conifers such as *Junipers* and *Pines* have interesting textures. Many of the succulents, *Scented Geraniums, Lamb's Ears, Paperbark Tree, Red Fountain Grass Mexican Bush Sage* and *Cork Oak* have leaves, flowers, or bark that are enticing to touch.

The aspects of a person's ch'i that represents the earth element are honesty, faith, trust, and integrity. Plants that represent these qualities are the *Fern,* which at one time was thought to bestow invisibility and is used medicinally to expel tapeworms; *Sweet Cicely* is known to aid in digestion; *Black Mustard* is seen growing in roadside areas everywhere. Who would guess this "weed" is used in plasters for inflammations as well as in table mustard? Other plants that are categorized with the element of earth are *Garden Anemone, Ivy, Elder, Balm of Gilead, Cedar, Cinquefoil, Cypress, Honeysuckle, Horehound, Jasmine, Pine, Sage,* and *Slippery Elm.*

Other Elements for the Center Area

There are many animals that also betoken longevity. Cicadas are considered by the Chinese to be symbols of immortality, eternal youth, and happiness. Jade cicadas were placed in the mouth of the deceased for memory after their passing and for a joyful next life. At the Botanical

Garden in Taipei, Taiwan, you see the cicada motif in the fence surrounding the garden. Rabbits are a token of longevity. The most ubiquitous symbol of longevity in the Chinese culture is

the Crane. Cranes are often paired together and with other longevity symbols such as Deer, Tortoise, and Pine. The Crane could also be placed in the Knowledge Gua as it is also symbolic of wisdom. The endless knot is one of the eight symbols of Buddhism and represents a long life that is uninterrupted by setbacks.

The crane is a symbol of longevity.

The center is an area concerned with stability and balance. In the Ba-Gua you see the Tai Chi, which is a symbol of perfect balance of yin and yang. You could also have plain stone paving, or this might be a good space to have a Japanese raked garden. These beautiful rock arrangements express the perfection of balance.

When More Is Too Much

In the desire to enhance an area or in the anxiety to attract a positive aspect to our lives, sometimes there is a misguided impulse to include everything that is suggested for a Gua to the exclusion of other elements. Another problem comes when people feel as though they must do everything suggested in every Gua. Balance of the elements as well as our lives is the key to happiness.

When our landscape is balanced with five senses, the five elements, and yin and yang, each season of the year will feel harmonious and stable. Using the suggestions in this chapter is a beginning point. Above all, it is most important to utilize your intuition and feelings in creating your landscape.

In the next chapter we will look at our properties from the outside in. If we don't look at the aspects of the land and the outside forces that affect a piece of property, we could miss important things that will affect our feng shui. Many of the solutions to issues that affect our daily lives will be revealed.

Chapter 6

From the Outside In

There are many things that your feng shui garden must do that the narrow focus of your property alone doesn't address. How does your house and property fit into the land, with the roads, the neighborhood, the city? We have already seen situations where lots or houses have missing pieces and have received good suggestions on how to fix the missing areas, but what about other situations? What effect does your house being close to the road have on you? Will being on a slope make you the master of all you see or will it condemn you to losing money or love? In this chapter we are going to look at how the exterior factors affect your feng shui.

One of the ways you can add energy to your life is by stemming the loss of ch'i. You can stop the loss of your personal ch'i by blocking or deflecting negative energy from your neighborhood. By correcting the problems with slopes or shapes of your land, blocks of ch'i to your home, and many other issues, you will have more energy available for your use. These are what are known as the *visible factors* to evaluate a piece of land.

In this chapter we will review the meaning and the common difficulties with the ch'i of the land, the shape of the lot, the shape of the house and what are called *exterior factors*.

Evaluating the Ch'i of Your Land

In rural China, where feng shui began, the best plots of land were midway up a hill between the protective arms of a mountain facing a river to the south. A house sited on land thus would be protected from the north winds and surprise attacks, take advantage of solar radiation, and have

Ill. 6-1. Here the land forms protect the house.

access to the life-sustaining properties of the water. It was best if the house site was on a smooth, gentle slope where agriculture was possible and roads or rivers accessing the property were easy. A house in this position isn't subject to cold, drafty night winds. At the top of the mountain, though the view may be more spectacular, the house has little protection from wind and other elements. If you are located in an area where there are hills or mountains, these same principles may still be employed. But many of us live in other situations.

Our cities are often flat or relatively flat landscapes. The features and buildings around us provide for us what the mountains and hills in China did. Do tall buildings protect your house from wind or create unpleasant wind tunnels? Do the adjacent trees encourage or block the sun and light to your house? Are the buildings around you overshadowing? If you are in a negative relationship to the elements around you, you may not feel effective in your life. You could feel overshadowed or overwhelmed.

How do you assess whether the energy of our land is sweet and abundant or scarce and dry? You could use your intuition, but because most of us are emotionally connected to our land, we can't be objective. Begin with looking at the plants. Where the foliage is green and lush, the ch'i is said to be at the surface and available for your use. On a property where the trees and plants are dying and the soil looks barren and dry, you will need to restore the land to restore the ch'i. Adding lights to the landscape can also increase the energy of the land.

Next, we can examine the people around us. Look around your neighborhood and see whether your neighbors keep their properties nicely or whether their front yard is a garbage heap. Are your neighbors nice or do you feel nervous around them?

Think about the events in the neighborhood. What has happened in the houses close to you? I once did a consultation for a client who had a serious illness. While we were standing at her front door she pointed out each and every house around her and told me of the tragedies that occurred in them, ranging from death, divorce, bankruptcy, illness, and accidents. This is an indicator of the ch'i of the land. If the land was a burial ground or there are present-day difficulties that have occurred in the vicinity, we need to adjust the energy there. In this case, I would recommend an exterior ch'i blessing ceremony, which we will review in the last chapter.

Another way to assess the ch'i of the land is to look at the animals that may come onto the property. Check with the Animals in Your Garden section in the next chapter to see whether an animal is lucky or not. For instance, if you go to see a house and there is a huge group of crows in the trees calling, that could be a warning against selecting that house. Likewise, if you come to a property and see a deer, it might be a very lucky or spiritual property. Animals may have messages for you about how ch'i could be shifting. So if you find that bats have taken up residence in your yard, if could be a message that prosperity lies ahead for you. On the other hand, if a black cat comes around howling at you, you may be in for an inauspicious event.

Finally, you can determine the ch'i of the land by observing spiritual occurrences. If you go to visit a potential home to buy and fall when you get out of the car or see a hearse pull up across the street, it is an omen that this might not be your dream house. On the other hand, if you pull up to a house and beautiful butterflies surround you or you find a C-note on the sidewalk, it may be a place that will bring you great joy or prosperity.

When feng shui masters speak about selecting a good site they consider sites for the dead as well as sites for the living. Sometimes the same places are lucky for both living and dead, and sometimes places are suitable for one and not the other. There may be certain types of places that are neither suitable for living nor dead. Let's consider the ten types of sites that you could choose to build a house or site a grave.

The first site to consider is <u>rough rock</u>. <u>Rough rock</u> (places that have more rock than dirt) is good for human habitation. As a yang residence (home or office) this site symbolizes stability, well-being, good health, and great potential and is especially good for factories or high-rises. It is as if the foundation of your business is as solid as a rock and therefore it has great potential. As a yin residence (grave site) this is not a good choice because the deceased will be deprived of inner peace and will take it out on their living relatives. This could lead to haunting, financial loss, and the general downfall of the site or to the relatives.

Let's look at a <u>wave-battered shore</u>. If you are living too close to the water and have it on both sides of you it is unsuitable for either human habitation or a resting place for the deceased. An illustration of this would be if the house is on an island or at the edge of the water with water all around it. Should this be the site of a factory, office, or business headquarters, business would decline and financial loss would ensue, leading to closure of the business. If you build apartments here, this would even be more dangerous. Accidents and other troubling developments would be frequent and whether used as yin or yang residence, those residing there would never enjoy peace of mind.

If you live near a <u>river, brook, or sewer</u>, it depends on if you live at the starting point, the middle, or the ending point whether your luck is good. For a house or business, the source of flowing water is good because where water begins the level of ch'i is high. Also, water symbolizes wealth and intelligence so those living on this site will enjoy financial prosperity, superior intelligence, and greater social status. Job promotions are in the picture and the person living here will eventually advance toward leadership or management. As a yin residence (burial ground) moisture is detrimental because it deprives the deceased of inner peace and therefore creates trouble and accidents for the living descendants or property owners.

Where a water flow comes to an end, the ch'i also comes to an end, so it is undesirable for both living and deceased. This location would bring bad luck and a general sense of decline. However, if the river ends in the ocean, there is great energy which will be excellent for living beings.

If you live near the middle of a river flow, in general it will have a positive effect on you; however, you need to assess the relationship of the river to your lot to get an accurate picture of the benefit or deficit. We will discuss various river shapes in relation to your lot when we look further at the exterior factors of energy.

A <u>lone hill</u> situation could be beneficial. As a yang residence (a house or office) it could be a superb site because you are sitting on the top of the world looking down. This location is suited to a leader of sorts, a head of state, or the top person of a particular field. For instance, if a person living here has dealings with the underworld, then he is likely to be a Mafia boss. This type of situation is good if you have the personality to carry it off. It may not be lucky if you don't like leadership positions. As a yin residence, it is not suited for individual burial. Should the deceased be buried here all alone, they will have no one and nothing to fall back on and will feel lonely and deserted. This in turn would create problems for their living relatives. If a cemetery is located here, it would be just fine.

Living <u>near a temple or church</u> can be difficult for the living, especially if it holds memorial or funeral services. The surroundings are unsuited for human habitation (be it home, office, or business) as the ch'i of death is too thick. If you already have a house near a church or temple, you can place a Ba-Gua mirror over your door to protect you from the yin forces of the neighborhood. As a yin residence, if the cemetery surrounds the church or temple, ghosts and spirits will feel that they are being protected and they will support their living relatives. If the cemetery is next to or directly across from a church or temple, then evil spirits will be misled into thinking that they can channel the power of the religious site. This will wreak havoc on the living. Hauntings and other ghostly occurrences will plague those living in the area. Within ten miles of a temple or church, you can get the yin ch'i of the deceased wandering around and creating havoc for their living neighbors.

If you are <u>surrounded by mountains on all sides</u>, it is not good for either the living or the deceased as you will feel as though you are a prisoner on the site.

Also, if you are <u>surrounded by jagged or disorderly hills</u>, it is not a place that is supportive of the living or the dead.

We say the site has an <u>air of sadness</u> when the scenery is desolate and deserted. Such a place is suitable neither for human habitation nor grave site. Should the wind howl like a weeping human, then the family that lives here will experience many tragedies such as suicide and loss of livelihood.

A <u>site with an undersized base</u> is one that doesn't provide support. For instance, the ground on which the house is constructed could be hollow underneath, the lot might be too small or low, or, difficult to access or disappearing. Such a site is not good for living or dead. If you live here your children will lose support and you will lose money and support.

At the crest of a hill you may experience one or two situations. If the top of the hill is round and broad, then it is suitable for both habitation and graves. If the peak is sharp and angular, then it is an undesirable site with strongly harmful ch'i. Both living and deceased on this site will not have a moment of peace. They will be plagued by illness, injury, death, continuous illness, and sudden death.

The Shape of the Lot

Most of us have lots that are square or rectangular. These are positive because in reviewing the Ba-Gua we realize that these shapes are "complete." A rectangular lot that is longer than it is wide is better for the flow of ch'i but neither case needs any correction.

There are many flag-shaped lots. When you place the Ba-Gua on such a lot you see that there are large missing areas. To correct this type of lot, you can plant around the missing area as illustrated in 6-2 to "fill in" the missing area with vitality. Another solution for this lot is to place spotlights in the two corners along the missing side and shine them at the highest point of the house. A third solution is to place a convex mirror in the missing corner to pull the complete shape into the missing area of the lot.

A triangular or pie shaped lot has problems, as you can see if you place the Ba-Gua on it. It is missing most of the back and that can't bode well for relationships or prosperity. There are many different ways that you can cure this lot and your fortune with it. Place lights at each of the front corners shining into the lot or a light at the back corner shining to the center of the lot. A decorative option would be to place three flags in the back corner or you could plant nine bamboos in the back corner.

A purse-shaped lot is one that has parallel front and back property lines and has the front of the property narrower than the back. When you place the Ba-Gua on this property you can see an extension in both Relationship and Wealth. This type of lot will foster a happy marriage and prosperity. Resources can pour in from all directions.

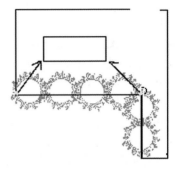

Ill 6-2 A flag lot can be corrected with lights or plants.

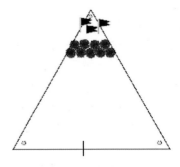

6-3 Triangular or Pie-Shaped Lot

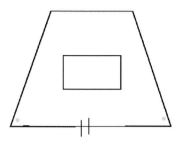

Ill. 6-4 Dustpan Shaped Lot is Unlucky

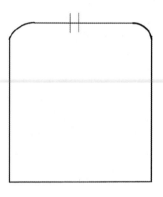

Ill. 6-5 Crab Shell Shaped Lot is very lucky

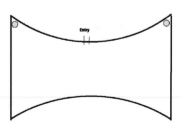

Ill. 6-6 Arced Entry Lot needs correction

The dust pan-shaped lot is just the opposite. It is wide at the front and narrow in the back so that when the Ba-Gua is superimposed you have missing Marriage and Wealth Guas. To cure this lot, place two lights at the entry corners (front of the lot) and shine them to the roof of the house.

A trapezoid-shaped lot has no parallel lines. The ones we are most concerned with are ones that have one side property line longer than the other. One of the main concerns with this type of lot is that the male side of the lot and the female side of the lot are not equal. Let me explain. If you are standing on the inside of a lot facing to the front, the right side is the male side and the left side is the female side. When one of those sides is smaller than the other, the people with the short side will suffer. So if your left side is shorter, females don't do well in this situation and if the right side is shorter, men won't thrive while living in this lot. In analyzing this kind of lot using the Ba-Gua you will note that one important corner will be missing. Again, there are many ways you can correct this kind of lot. If your lot is extremely large you could erect a fence to square off the lot or you could place a light in the short corner to expand it or a convex mirror in the short corner to draw in the long side so that they are equal.

Another shape of lot is known as the crab shell shape. This is one that is rounded at the front and wide at the back. This is one that brings great prosperity to the residents.

If you enter a lot on the arc that is arced in the front and back, you need to make corrections to it. You can do this by placing two spotlights at the corners of the entry line and shine them to the roof of the house. See illustration 6-6. The same shaped lot with the entry on the flat ends does not require feng shui adjustment.

Some lots have none of these shapes and rather are odd shaped. Look at the shape of an odd-shaped lot with your intuition. What does it remind you of? Do you get any inspiration when you first see it? For example, you may see a lot that resembles a clam. This could be extremely lucky, especially if your house is in the center, which is the power point or strong muscle area of the clam. Another example is a lot that resembles a Bamboo Pen Holder which again is lucky and especially good for scholars.

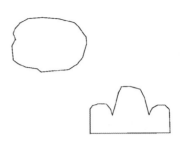

Ill. 6-7 Clam Shape, left; Bamboo Pen Holder, right

The slope of your land is important too. If your house sits on a slope above the street, this is generally lucky because your personal energy lifts each day as you go up to the house. This reminds me of the question that many people ask about the relationship of the feng shui of the inside of the house as it relates to the outside. What if your home is in a very favorable feng shui position from the outside but is a feng shui nightmare on the inside? I have seen both interior difficulties and exterior difficulties. The closer the living space is to you, the more it affects you. So, if your bedroom has great feng shui but your yard is horrible, it won't have as great an effect as the other way around. I had a client who lived in a perfect exterior situation. The house sat up the slope from the street and across the street was a beautiful lake and park. But, just at the front door there were three major feng shui difficulties. The client met their soul mate while living in this house but also experienced several difficult health problems which resolved themselves upon moving.

If, however, your house is on a slope below the street, the opposite is true; your energy declines as you enter the house. The effect of living below the street may be unpleasant changes in your life or loss of money. The most effective solution to remedy land that slopes away from your house is to place two spotlights at the bottom of the hill shining to the top of the roof. This re-circulates the energy from the bottom of the hill back up to the house where it nourishes you.

Evaluating Your Land

Check boxes that apply:

Needs No Correction	May Need Correction
__ House is midway up a gentle hill protected by arms of mountains	__ At the top of mountain or on a steeply sloped hill
__ On flat land with a house in a homogeneous neighborhood	__ On flat land with much taller buildings all around
__ On a straight street with moderate traffic or with traffic coming toward you	__ On a very busy street close to the house
__ In the middle of the block	__ At the end of a T intersection or cul-de-sac
__ Square or rectangular lot	__ Odd-shaped lot
__ Plant life flourishing	__ Trees and plants dying or not existent
__ Friendly, prosperous neighbors	__ Unfriendly or strange neighbors
__ Homogeneous neighborhood with mostly houses and small businesses	__ Cemeteries, mortuaries, churches, dumps facing or near your house
__ Buildings around you oriented in the same direction	__ Corner of a house or building pointed at your house.
__ Street is well lit and safe	__ Street lights are harshly lighting your property or telephone pole is within view

Shape of the House

The shape of the house is another aspect that affects your life. Cures to correct the feng shui of a house are traditionally done inside the home but many wonderful corrections can be done outside as well. The square and rectangular shaped houses require no correction.

If you have a missing area of your home, whichever section is missing will cause missing potential in that part of your life. If you want to make the correction for the area you can add a tree at the confluence of the corner or a light, a fountain, or a flag.

One of the common missing shaped houses is one that is known as the Chinese Lock Shape. This shape is particularly troublesome if the kitchen, dining room, or master bedroom is in one of the rooms that protrude in front of the front door. We have been given many solutions to this shaped house over the years. One of the most effective solutions was given to me by my mentor, Katherine Metz, who suggested that I hang a wind chime in the empty area and place a bell at each of the four corners of the house. Another solution would be to place brick planters on both sides of the opening to "complete" the shape. Finally, a highly recommended option would be to paint a red line from corner to corner using red paint with cinnabar powder in it to complete the shape. Don't mistake this shape for an interior courtyard. When there is a courtyard inside the center of the house, especially if there is water and greenery, it can be very good for luck. The important element if there is an interior courtyard is that it must be accessed by an interior door. If it only has windows into the space it could portend someone in the house going to prison.

Many of our modern houses have an L shape. This can either be in plan view or elevation. These shapes create missing areas to the Ba-Gua, and especially if they are a boot or cleaver shape they could present other problems for you if you sleep on the toe or heel, enter the home in those areas, or if the kitchen is located in those areas. With a cleaver-shaped house, if those sensitive areas are on the knife edge of the cleaver, it could be detrimental to your health and wealth. Let's examine several landscape methods to solve the problem. Many boot-shaped houses are the result of adding a large garage in the front of a rectangular home. The walkway to the front door usually comes from the driveway around the garage to the entry. If the garage takes up more than 1/2 the width of the house, it is out of proportion and needs to be adjusted. To create balance in this situation, you can add a path or stepping stones that lead from the front door to the far corner of the yard.

Another common house configuration is when a circular driveway brings your car almost to your front door and then out. To remedy this situation, you canplace a pond or fountain in the center or the driveway. Remember to direct the water toward the front door.

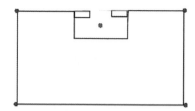

Ill. 6-8 Chinese Lock Shape

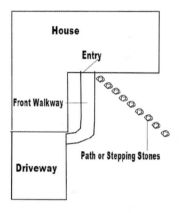

Ill. 6-9 Boot-Shaped example 1

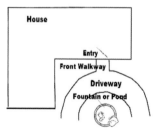

Ill. 6-10 Boot-Shaped example 2

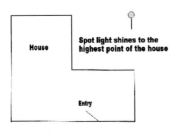

Ill. 6-11 Boot Shaped example 3

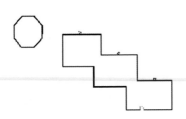

Ill. 6-12 Lightning Bolt Shaped House

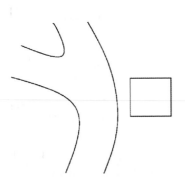

Ill. 6-13 Street Curving away and Crossroad at upper right

A third situation is when the missing area is in the backyard. The best solution is to place a spotlight in the back shining toward the highest point of the house. An unusual solution would be to make a planter near the heel of the boot and run vines from the planter to the top of the boot to transcendentally take the pressure off the toe of the boot. Sometimes the plan view shape of the house is rectangular but the elevation of the house is a boot. In this situation you could grow vines from the ground to the top of the boot to take the pressure off of the toe of the boot.

When the house has a small entry that protrudes in front of the elevation of the house this small nose limits the flow of energy into the house. To correct this you can add plants on both sides of the nose to add vitality and expand the entry.

One relatively unusual house shape is the lightning bolt shape. It is one that steps back in both the front and the back like a lightning bolt. This can be a dynamic and powerful home if you know how to adjust it to your advantage. You can add lights to the back, which is like the spine of the dragon. The brightest light is at the head, with each light dimmer as you move away from the head. To add more power, if you have space, you can add a gazebo at the head of the dragon.

Outside Your Property

Once you have fixed all that you can on your property we need to look around at the factors exterior to your property to see how they can be mitigated through your garden. Among the most important relationships to the outside world is the road. In rural China rivers were and are the lifeblood to people. They carry trade that brings prosperity and provide water to irrigate crops. In modern cities, most of us don't live near such a beneficial feature. Our rivers are the asphalt streets that bring us to and from work, and provide routes for our livelihood. Most of our city streets are in straight lines, which is a neutral force except when a home is at the terminus of the street, the T intersection, or a dead end. In this situation you are at the effect of energy coming forcefully straight toward you. To correct the damage of this situation, hang a concave mirror over your front door.

Where the streets are curved, you need to be mindful of where your house is placed. A street that curves around you will bring prosperity. If you would like to create the good energy of the curved street while your house is on a straight street you can create a planting bed or river rocks that curve around the house.

A house that is on the outside curve of the street creates energy where we may see profits but not be able to acquire or hold them. You can use a convex mirror to embrace all parts of a road that curves away from you. A house with its main entrance facing a road curving outwards and a crossroads on the upper right may bring lawsuit, bankruptcy, disease, and self-destruction to its inhabitants. Again, the solution is a convex mirror over the door to pull the money into the house and keep it from leaving. If you have a crossroad and an intersection in front of the house, then the residents of this house are likely to develop a similar fate to the previous situation. The solution to this road interface is to add a weathervane with an arrow faced to point toward the offending street.

A house near an abandoned house or a house which has perpendicular roads running into its front and back entrances can bring mysterious illnesses or a lawsuit or finance problems to its inhabitants. The solution is to either add weathervanes pointing back at the offending streets or add a Ba-Gua mirror over the front door. A road that resembles a pitch fork where the handle is at the front door signifies a dispute between generations. A Ba-Gua mirror over the front door will resolve the issue.

Many of us in suburbia live on cul-de-sacs. In a cul-de-sac energy comes in and pools with no outlet. The energy here may stagnate

This shows the worst position in a cul-de-sac. Not only do you have stagnate energy but the street opposes the house.

and the most common effect is problems with neighbors. I have had a few clients in this situation and have seen how either people are attached to their neighbor's business or there is hidden hostility that shows its colors at inopportune times. A strategically placed water wheel in the front yard, windsock, or whirligig can keep the energy circulating and thus alleviate the problem. If the cul-de-sac has a center island, you could place a fountain or a flag in the center of it to shift the energy for all of the neighbors in the cul-de-sac.

Bridges in your neighborhood must also be analyzed. If you have a bridge that confronts your front door or your house, it can be more dangerous than a road because of its three-dimensional nature. The closer it is to you, the more dangerous. If there are houses between you and the bridge, the effect is not as severe. To adjust the energy you can use a concave mirror over your front door. If you have a bridge leading to your house on your property and it is solid and sturdy, no adjustment is needed.

Rivers are treated the same way as roads. That is, if they embrace the house it is a positive situation and if the river bows away from the house, you would want to place a convex mirror to pull all sides of the river into favorable relationship to the house. As stated before, if you live at the beginning or the middle of the river course, it is a positive relationship for you, while at the end of the river, the ch'i is weak and won't nourish you. If your house is actually over a river, there will be a great deal of instability and you will never find peace of mind. This is also true if you have an underground river flowing under your property. To adjust the energy you can plant nine bamboos in each of the four corners of the property.

There are many aspects of our neighborhood or neighbors that can act as a drain on us. For instance, if our house faces a tunnel it may act as a drain siphoning away our energy. An abandoned house or building nearby can drain or divert our energy. Buildings that house or formerly housed violence, illness, or death such as a police station, an old fort, a hospital, or a mortuary that is seen on the way home daily can affect us negatively. Even churches, which hold funerals, may be a negative source of energy. Although churches also have positive events, the negative ones can drain the ch'i from the neighborhood. There may be subtle and common every-day depletion of our energy such as a water hydrant in front of our front door, a sewer drain, or a pedestrian crossing. More obvious drains on energy are being in the field of airplane traffic or, being close to a microwave station, television transmission station, or a sewage pond. A location close to railroad tracks, because of the noise and fast-moving ch'i, can bring instability to your health and wealth. The best way to protect you and your home from potential wandering spirits from the church or temple or any of these other negative factors is to place a Ba-Gua mirror over the front door.

If you live on a corner it is likely that the house catty corner will have a corner pointing in your direction, sending poison arrows your way. This can cause friction in the neighborhood. A roof ridge pointing in your direction can be equally as devastating. This situation is particularly harsh if the arrow is pointed at your front door or your master bedroom. To cure this situation you can either use a Ba-Gua mirror over your front door or plant plants between the offender and your house. Also, if there is a telephone pole nearby it could foster incessant lawsuits, illnesses, or children problems. One solution with the telephone pole is to plant nine bamboos between the house and the pole. Nine bamboos can also protect your home from high-voltage power lines, transformer boxes, transmission towers, or garbage dumps in your neighborhood. For telephone poles or pillars that feel oppressive you can also hang protector deities such as Earth Gods or protector deities from your own religious sensibilities on the offensive object.

We have already mentioned the negative effect of tall buildings that tower over you and overshadow your house or apartment. I once lived in a condominium in Los Angeles where a high-rise building's corner (poison arrow) pointed directly at our building complex. My relatively new building was subsequently demolished so that the new subway could be built. To negate the pressure from a tall building near you, you can place a concave mirror over your front door or on your roof pointing at the building. Concave mirrors take images and turn them upside down so that you are neutralizing the negative energy coming at you.

In the next chapter I will discuss more about the entry to your home but in this section I want you to know about some general principles and unusual cases. The driveway and entry walk should have an open, generous, grand feeling. It is important to avoid narrow, constricted pathways to the front door. Plants that crowd or overwhelm the walkway should be cut back or removed. Plants that have sword-like leaves or thorns should also be avoided because they can be a source of harsh energy as you enter or leave your house each day. If you feel a strong affinity or love for such plants, be sure their leaves are pointed straight up or that they are located somewhere away from the main entry path or driveway or their thorns are not so close that you will be pricked on the way home.

A road or path leading to the door which resembles the Chinese symbol / \ where the point of the symbol is toward the front door is likely to support rebellious offspring.

If the entry path is wider at the house than it is at the street or sidewalk there could be an abrupt ending to the main source of income. Where clients don't want to replace their front walk, I have often designed flower beds that widen at the sidewalk to welcome positive energy and income into the property.

If a front walkway resembles the Chinese number seven, which looks like the letter t, it can portend great riches as long as all of the crosses are straight. If the t is wiggly it can resemble a dead duck and then there will be daily disputes.

If you were to design a walkway in the shape of the Chinese coins and attach them either physically or symbolically, you could bring riches into your home. I have seen this motif accomplished in a few different ways. In later chapters I will describe and show you the ones I have designed.

This chapter dealt with the view from outside the property. It is important to be aware of how to fix unlucky and negative aspects of the exterior world. A few chapters ago we reviewed design elements from the point of view of the Ba-Gua. In the next chapter we will view the design elements themselves to give you some guidelines for their use.

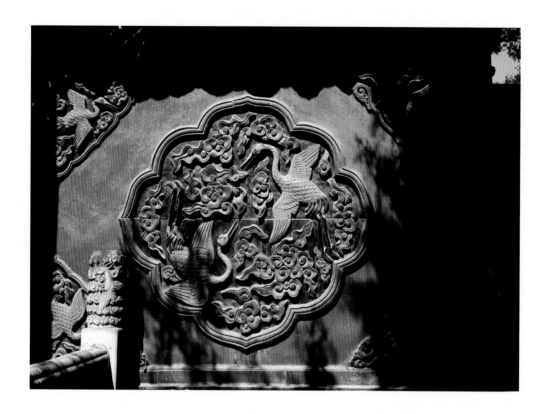

Chapter 7

Playing in the Garden with Design Elements

We all have many choices when designing the garden. Should we plant a Willow or a Pine tree? What plants should we use along our walkway? What shape and material are best for the walkway? There are so many elements that we can introduce into our garden to make it more meaningful and lucky. This chapter will review plants, animals, and hardscape elements such as fences, paving, driveways, pools, and more. Feng shui can help us make some of these choices while giving us support for particular areas of our lives.

Plants are the easiest and most interesting change you can make in the garden. They are the key to your deepest connection. To narrow down your selection, you could review folklore of the plants, specifically the feng shui effects of plants on your properties. Whether you love plants for their sensual pleasures, for their legends, or from childhood memories, all you need is love to include them.

Trees, Trees, Trees

A landscape architect almost always begins with the trees since they are usually the framework and the backbone for a design. Often trees define the color palette or the theme for the garden. Their location and size determine the amount of shade that is offered in the lot, home, and plants. When you want to add trees to the lot, think about all of these factors and assess how much yang or light you need and how much yin or shade you need to balance your environment and house.

In addition to these considerations, you may want to look back at the Ba-Gua assessment and see if you want to add elements of the Ba-Gua to any particular area of the lot. In terms of feng shui, trees are extremely important because they can help root you to a place. Compared to other plants, tree roots are deep and help to lift the ch'i of the earth from the earth to the heavens. Adding trees is one of the easiest ways that you can reverse the loss of ch'i on a property.

In choosing a tree there are certain feng shui considerations to keep in mind. The first is that evergreen trees are preferable to deciduous trees. This brings me to an interesting point. As a landscape architect I often suggest a deciduous tree for a sunny side of a house so that it will cool in summer and warm in the winter to support the environment and my client's energy bills. When I am asked to consult on the same property for feng shui, I may not make the same suggestion. The same dilemma can also present itself in a home where I am consulted for feng shui. While most of the feng shui choices are environmentally sound and aesthetically pleasing, occasionally they are not and when the reason for adjusting the feng shui is important, I will always err on the side of good energy, which outweighs the other factors.

Another principle in selecting trees is that upward facing leaves are preferable to downward facing leaves. Again in terms of lifting the energy of a property, leaves pointing up lifts energy up while leaves pointing down can drag the ch'i down. I had one client, upon examining the leaf of a weeping Ficus tree, remark that the stem and leaves resembled a person hanging by the neck.

A tree that has flowers or fruits is preferable to a tree with no flowers or fruits. Flowering trees offer us the chance to introduce color, scent, and texture to the garden. Because flowering trees attract bees and birds, they also can bring pleasant sounds to the garden. That is another way of introducing the five elements to the garden and balancing the energy on the property. Fruits, as I have said before, produce abundance wherever they are on your property.

Trees have a particularly powerful energy. An old tree that has been worshipped, loved, and positively regarded becomes an incredibly powerful force. Communicating with it can bring you good luck and maybe special messages. This is true because the tree's root, which sinks deep into the earth, has access to ch'i that is primordial and pure. I learned about communicating with trees many years ago from shamanic teachers and have been surprised at the extent and variety of information that has been given to me over the years. The most stunning piece of information that came to me was in mid-1993. I was meditating at the major tree on my property. I was told that I had to sell the house and leave. I was so shocked and though the message was very clear, I didn't sell. How could I tell my husband, who loved the house, that the tree told us to move? Six months later when the 1994 Northridge earthquake hit we had to move immediately and lost a great deal of money on the property.

There are several different methods to communicate with your trees or plants. In my shamanic training, I was taught to sit with my back to a tree on each of the cardinal sides of the tree. After practicing that way for several years, I naturally started to place my hands and forehead on the tree. Several years ago on a trip to China, I learned about just placing hands on the tree to retrieve messages.

Let's look at some of the trees that might be worshipped or positively regarded. The *Firmiana simplex,* known in China as the Wutong Tree is thought to be the only perch for the phoenix. The Chinese phoenix is a symbol of high virtue and grace, appearing only when reason prevails in the country. It is a benevolent creature that feeds only on bamboo seeds. It is considered a symbol of the female element, the opposite of the bamboo, which symbolizes the male element.

Five trees that symbolize different stations in life are often planted at gravesites. These trees have such power that they are said to lift the spirit of the deceased. The tree for rulers is the *Pinus* or Pine Tree. The *Thuja* or Arborvitae gets its common name from the Tree of Life. It is planted in gravesites for princes and is a long-lived tree with a very sturdy appearance. It is used in disinfectants, cleansers, and insecticides. *Koelreuteria bipinnata* or Chinese Flame Tree represents governors. This tree has lovely yellow flowers in the spring followed by papery capsules resembling Chinese lanterns in red, orange, and salmon colors. The capsules are used in flower arrangements. The *Sophora japonica,* Chinese Scholar Tree, represents scholars and has been used for its yellow dye and ability to fight and treat cancer. The *Populus,* Poplar Tree, represents commoners. It is interesting how Poplar wood has been revered in different areas of the world. It is said that the Poplar Tree wood was used for the cross of Jesus and in America has been used by indigenous cultures for the Sundance ceremony.

Trees are often said to contain spirits in addition to their own powerful energy. The *Ginkgo biloba,* Maidenhair tree, is most important, as it is said to contain the spirit of Buddha or Bodhisattvas. The national tree of China, it has been used medicinally to thin the blood and to assist dementia patients.

Probably the most revered trees in Buddhist religion are the *Ficus religiousa*, the Bodhi Tree, under which Buddha was born and became enlightened. Thus, the Bodhi Tree is a well-known symbol for happiness, prosperity, longevity and good luck.

On a lighter note, *Palm Trees* are planted throughout temperate climates and loved by many. I have used Palm trees because of their windmill look to lift the energy on properties. Palm trees can indicate that your style of seeking answers is stubborn, so if your next door neighbors have palm trees, they might be difficult. The Palm has been an important tree in many cultures. It is said to be a symbol of victory and riches and is the emblem of light. If a Palm Tree has a white vine climbing on it, it indicates nagging problems that won't go away. The solution is to tie nine red ribbons onto the vine to alleviate the nagging problems. Removing the vine would be a mundane solution. If you do that, it is a good solution but you would still need the nine ribbons to cleanse the energy.

Plants and Their Meanings

This section is devoted to the Chinese meanings of different plants. There are suggestions for the use of some of these plants. There are cautions on where to avoid some of them and how to minimize their negative effects.

The *Apple Tree* stands for safety. Placing an Apple Tree in the front of your home may safeguard the house. In the Wealth area it provides safety for your resources. It is also good for your health, as in "an apple a day." Apples are often placed on altars as a wish for safety of the family.

The *Apricot, Cherry Blossom,* and *Peach Trees* individually have many positive symbolisms. The Peach Tree is said to carry fruit from which immortality is granted. Cherry Blossoms are said to mirror the transient nature of beauty and life as their blossoms delight us and then fade and die. All of these trees, if planted in your neighbor's yard and grow over into your yard, are a sign of unwanted sexual advances or other problems of a romantic nature. The solution to this is a transcendental ceremony. Mix a teaspoon of realgar and a pinch of cinnabar powder with 99 drops from a newly opened high-proof liquor bottle. Use your middle finger to dip into the mixture and flick it nine times at the branches that are reaching in. Perform the Three Secret Reinforcement as described in Chapter 4, visualizing that the disaster will be averted. If you have planted an Apricot, Cherry Blossom, or Peach Tree too close to your property edge so that it extends to your neighbor, it is a sign of either male or female marital infidelity. There is a transcendental cure to counteract this problem as well. The stability cure should be done for the husband and wife. To do this, cut a piece of new red paper into a three-inch round. With a new black pen, while holding your breath, write the word DING (which means calm or stability or safety) on one side, and continuing to hold your breath, the person's name and birth date on the back side. Put the paper between the box spring and mattress of the bed under the person's heart area with the writing "DING" facing down.

Artemesia or Wormwood protects against evil spirits. It has often been hung over the door at the time of the Dragon Boat Festival (which is the fifth day of the fifth Lunar month) to repel insects that are active during this time.

Azaleas, while much beloved and cherished by gardeners for their beauty in shady conditions, are often associated with blood illnesses and sad memories. The key here is not to have exclusively azaleas in your plant palette. Also, red azaleas are more inauspicious than white, orange, or pink azaleas.

Bamboo represents fidelity, wisdom, and longevity. They also symbolize flexibility and the ability to cooperate with others.

The *Banana Tree* represents scholarly ambitions and cultivation. Penniless scholars would often practice their calligraphy on its leaves in an effort to advance in a society that rewarded scholars regardless of their background. If there is a pregnant woman in the home, it is best to cover the *Banana Tree* until after the healthy birth.

Cactus symbolizes persevering and even thriving through adversity. Be careful where it is planted because it can be detrimental if close to walkways or near the front door.

Camellia represents evergreen, relaxation, and longevity. It is a shade-loving plant that brings us its beautiful flowers throughout the winter.

Cherry Trees are a good tree to use about anywhere. As with any fruit tree, they are particularly potent when used in the Wealth corner.

Chrysanthemums represent longevity, gentility, and elegance. Symbols of the sun, the Japanese consider the orderly unfolding of the chrysanthemum's petals to represent perfection. Confucius suggested they be used as an object of meditation. In China, Japan, and Korea, as well as many Western countries the white chrysanthemum is symbolic of grief so when creating bouquets, you want to avoid using only chrysanthemums or using too many light-colored chrysanthemums in your garden.

Columbine is good for love and romance but be careful of the potential for fickleness in love with this plant.

Daylily is good for maternal love, maternity, and fertility. The flower is called "Wong Yu," meaning "Forgetting Worries." The flower is worn by many mothers so it is venerated as a symbol of filial devotion to one's mother. This makes it a great plant to put in the Children's area or the Marriage corner. The Daylily is used in cooking as it is edible in all its parts.

Ferns are used as protection from ghost invasions. They are another wonderful shade plant that provides texture and beauty to the landscape composition.

Grapes are sour. They are not as good as other fruiting plants and they represent jealousy.

Hibiscus represents the early morning sun as a positive element but it also represents a family that has had a death. Therefore, use great caution when planting these. I don't normally recommend that clients add this to their gardens. If they feel they must have it then I recommend a single plant worked in with others. I try to keep them in the background or at the very least not near the entry to the house. If a property has Hibiscus and the owners are unwilling to remove them, you can use the transcendental adjustment of mixing cinnabar with uncooked rice and newly opened high-proof liquor and spread the mixture around the *Hibiscus,* visualizing that the energy of the plant is contained and that disaster will be averted. If your neighbor's *Hibiscus* hedge adjoins your property you can plant a *Quince Tree* or *Bamboo* to protect your property.

Holly represents happiness, longevity, and perseverance. It is a beautiful plant that adds the great red berries and dark green leaves that have come to symbolize Christmas. In European cultures it symbolizes the winter season.

Kumquats represent auspiciousness and that things in life will go smoothly. At Chinese New Year they are given as a wish for a smooth and lucky year.

Lemon Trees represent spirit and stimulation. Planting them in any area will stimulate the energy and bear fruit.

Few flowers are more beloved than the *Lotus.* It represents purity, wisdom, and compassion. In the Buddhist philosophy the marriage of wisdom with compassion is what allows the ethereal concept of love to be tempered with the reality of our human condition.

Morning Glory can wake up those who are low in spirit and uplift those that are unclear. It is almost as if its trumpet sounds. The flowers are so beautiful and mesmerizing to look at, but my job as a landscape architect wouldn't be done if I didn't warn you about the invasiveness of this plant. I have rarely specified it because it can be such a nuisance.

The *Mulberry Tree* is crucial to the silk industry in China. It is the tree that feeds the silkworm and has brought much prosperity and attention to many in China, so you may be surprised to learn that you should not have a *Mulberry Tree* in the front of your house or it could lead to financial ruin. This is because the leaves are always eaten by the silkworms. This tree located in the backyard is fine. Chinese Taoists considered this tree to predate the separation of yin and yang in the universe and therefore it represents cosmic order.

The *Narcissus* represents good fortune and good fate. As I have mentioned, if you have a blooming *Narcissus* in your home during Chinese New Year it is said to bring you luck for the entire year.

Olive Trees represent peace. It is interesting to see this cross-cultural meaning of the tree. It loves the sun and warmth and is another fruiting tree so is good luck wherever it is planted.

Chinese restaurants often serve oranges for dessert. The *Orange Tree* is considered to be good luck so every time you receive that sweet dessert, it is a wish for good luck. You can place an *Orange Tree* wherever you need more luck.

Orchids represent the qualities of a gentleman - nobility, culture and graciousness. They therefore can be added to your Partnership area, especially if you are seeking a mate with those attributes.

Peach and *Plum Trees* represent brotherliness, charm and friendship. The Plum Tree blooms at the end of winter to beginning spring. The brotherliness and friendship qualities come from the two important groups that the Plum Tree belongs to. It is one of the three friends of the cold along with the Pine and Bamboo, which show their resilience and perseverance through the adversity of winter. The other friendly group is the Four Gentlemen of Flowers, which represents the concept of nobility. Besides the Plum Tree the four friends are *Orchid, Chrysanthemum,* and *Bamboo.* In addition, the Plum Blossom is the winter flower of the four seasons.

The *Pear Tree* is symbolic of your health and your heart so be careful not to split the fruit. When you are eating it with a group of people it represents health and safety. It also has meaning in different cultures; for instance, it is included in a popular Christmas song and in Europe was often planted when a baby girl was born as a special blessing for her.

Peonies have many different honors attached to them; luck, prosperity, honor, aristocracy, and wealth. In addition, they are intensely fragrant as well as beautiful to behold. They were the national flower of China. Naturally, they can be placed in the Career area, Wealth area, Fame area, or anywhere else you would like these attributes.

Persimmons represent joy, luck in business, and a good start for a new endeavor. As such, they would be an excellent choice for the Career area or the Wealth area. Because they are among the luckiest trees, they can bring luck to wherever they are planted.

Much has already been said about the *Pine Tree,* which represents resilience, integrity, dignity, and longevity. I have already suggested its use in many different sections of the Ba-Gua and it can be used wherever you would like to manifest the qualities it represents.

Pomegranate Trees, because of their many seeds, represent fertility. They can be used in the Children's area to foster fertility or the Marriage Gua, which supports the part of the body governing fertility. I have one client who attributes her children to this tree alone.

The *Quince Tree,* because of its tolerance of cold weather carries, the attribute of perseverance. Quince is grown as much for its beautiful fragrant flowers as its fruit.

Rose, as has been mentioned before, is a sign of love or romance. The thorns that are part of this plant indicate the potential problems that are inherent in that aspect of life. Be careful not to plant roses too near walkways and entries. Although they look wonderful lining a sidewalk, if they are treacherous, your career and life could go in that direction as well.

Sunflower stands for strength, power, and loyalty. These are particularly good qualities to have in Career but are excellent for any of the other areas of the property. The flower is considered to be particularly yang so it could serve to balance a white or purple area of the garden. The yang quality will also help motivate you if you are struggling with depression.

Water hyacinth symbolizes beauty and grace and so is a likely choice for a Relationship area. Like the *Lotus.* this plant lives only in the water so it is a good choice for a pond or a water pot. They multiply freely so take care not to release it in a public waterway where they are an invasive species.

The *Weeping Willow* symbolizes grace but again, planted in the backyard, it could bring you sorrow. It is particularly associated with people making wrong use of your talents or a spouse slipping away. Chinese legend has this tree playing a major part in a tragic story of a woman who leaves her father's home with her true love after being engaged to another man. The story ends in sorrow for all involved.

Sometimes I think wherever there are plants there are plant meanings to help people. You can also look for plants' healing purposes in Chinese medicinal herbs or Bach remedies. Use your intuition and artistry to put the right plant in the right place.

Animals in Your Garden

You can integrate animals into your landscape in several different ways. Of course, the easiest way is to invite them to your home such as a pet or with bird feeders, plants, or housing. You can also have representative art such as murals or have carvings of them.

Domesticated animals are the ones you are more likely to invite into your home. Cats are generally considered good luck because they dispel evil spirits wherever they go. They also go where the food is good so they are good fortune. The exception to this is black cats that are considered inauspicious. Beware when a cat disappears from your house as it could be a sign that the good ch'i has left as well.

Dogs represent loyalty so they also are considered lucky; even more so than cats. They bring fidelity and prosperity with them. That is why they are in Chinese folklore terms more desirable than cats. Watch out for stray yellow dogs that are considered unlucky.

Horses represent speed, success, and perseverance. Their near relative the Donkey represents stupidity.

Pigs represent good fortune. Despite these qualities good feng shui doesn't support using representations of pigs, ox, or sheep in landscape design. These animals are considered beasts of burden and our slaves so are not suitable in the landscape design.

Wild animals can freely be used in landscape design. In China I often saw representations of animals in the paving patterns, carved into railings, or painted on overhead structures.

Though I have no desire to see the Ant anywhere, even in a representation on my property, it represents virtue and patriotism. A friend of mine just told me that ants will go to great lengths to protect those related to them. The closer the relation, the greater lengths they will go to serve.

Bears represent bravery, strength, and luck. In mountain resorts I have often seen the stumps of dead trees turned into powerful bear statues.

Deer are considered to be very lucky. They are associated with the four enjoyments of life, which are happy events, promotion, longevity, and good fortune. The Chinese word for deer has the elements of each. Deer are said to be the only animal capable of finding the Fungus of Immortality so they also represent longevity. In the Buddhist tradition the deer has special meaning. It is said that Buddha in a past life as a deer committed a highly unselfish act that saved many lives. When he started preaching, the park where he taught was called Deer Park.

The Elephant has held a fascination for many of the Eastern cultures because they are considered lucky. In India the elephant was the mount of rulers. The Hindu god Ganesh has the head of an elephant and is said to help overcome obstacles and invite in prosperity. Chinese culture attributes energy, strength, and power to them. In Buddhism they are a symbol of patience and wisdom because they represent the future Buddhas with the ability to grant wishes.

The Fox is thought of as a supernatural animal because it could bring messages from the dead. They represent longevity and craftiness. They are said to have ability at age fifty to assume the form of a woman and at one hundred a young and beautiful girl or a wizard. In their woman form they can cause great mischief so there is a healthy respect for the fox.

The Monkey is a popular animal in the Chinese culture, representing success. They can protect people by driving away evil influences. They are also included in the list of "Three Senseless Creatures": the tiger for always being angry, the deer for always being lovesick, and the monkey who is always grabbing at things. Nevertheless, monkeys have been treasured in China. Their skin was so valuable that only members of the imperial family could wear it.

The Rabbit or Hare represents longevity since it was thought to live to 1,000. The Rabbit was believed to have come from the essence of the moon and some dynasties thought that the Rabbit lived on the moon's surface.

Rats are active at night and steal food from the storage bin and so are symbolic of scoundrels. In ancient times they were considered disease-bearing thieves. If you raise them and feed them, you are feeding scoundrels and that ch'i may incubate. Someone may come back to haunt you. Because they locate, acquire, and save abundant supplies they also represent industry and prosperity. In Southern China, while the fox turns into a female demon, the rat turns into a male demon.

Reptiles are "scary" and not normally considered auspicious.

Snakes represent wisdom but also could be the haunting of a lost spirit. Snakes can also be wicked and treacherous. They are supposed to be very sensual creatures as well. In other cultures snakes represent resurrection because they can shed their skins and be reborn.

Tigers symbolize courage, majesty, dignity, fierceness, wealth, and protection. The Tiger is considered to be the lord of land animals the way the Dragon is the lord of the sea animals. He is fierce and protective so you often see the Tiger protecting people's houses or on their doorposts as a guard against demons. Sometimes the God of Wealth is shown as a Tiger or as riding a Tiger so it is also associated with wealth.

The wolf represents treachery and is associated with greed and cruelty. In some places it was customary to draw large white rings around the house to scare the wolf away.

Birds and bees are generally considered a very positive force in the landscape with a few exceptions. The lively nature and sound of animals in the yard bring vitality to whatever section they inhabit. I encourage you to add the elements that would attract these creatures-plants, housing such as trees or bat houses, and feeders. We will look at some of the birds and bees to see the omens they bring with them.

The Bat represents good luck. If you have bats on your property, they can bring you prosperity. The term for Bat, Fu, is close to the word for happiness. When you see a motif of five bats, it illustrates the Five Blessings: old age, wealth, health, love of virtue, and natural death.

As in Western traditions, the Bee represents industry and thrift.

The Butterfly symbolizes joy. It also represents marital happiness. When paired with a plum blossom the two represent long life and perfect beauty.

As discussed before, the Crane represents longevity and wisdom. I have seen many of these designed into the paving or railings. Two Cranes flying toward the sun represents the wish for you to "rise high." Cranes are said to transport immortal beings and so are often carved onto the face of coffins to convey a departed soul to heaven.

In the Chinese traditions one of the inauspicious birds is the Black Crow. This may come from the sound that they make, which is low and sad. It is considered an omen of evil maybe because its call sounds like the word for "bite," indicating that any business venture will not be successful.

Because they mate for life, Doves represent faithfulness and impartiality. The dove is also a fertility symbol as it is often seen in the headdress of Kuan Yin (Chinese Goddess of Mercy) who sends children.

Ducks, especially the Mandarin duck, represent marital fidelity. They are also a symbol of happiness when paired with the lotus. Duck amulets were often worn as a protection against drowning.

The Eagle, king of birds, is a symbol of strength and power of the United States. This emblem carries through to Western civilizations where Native Americans view it as an animal with mystical powers, a shuttle between heaven and earth.

Hawk represents authority. In America, the Hawk is a messenger from heaven as it awakens our communication to the heavens.

The Hummingbird is a messenger who delivers sweet, auspicious messages. In Native American cultures the Hummingbird stands for joy.

Magpie brings auspiciousness. The Chinese name sounds like the word for "happy events" so it often forecasts good news or the arrival of a guest. If they build their nest near your home you can expect great good fortune.

Because their call sounds like the digging of a grave, Owls represent death.

Parrots, or other birds that can mimic sounds, are auspicious. It is believed that they may have been human in their past life. Their frequency is close to that of the human and they may return in the next lifetime as a human being. One dares not to speak near the parrot because a parrot could repeat it.

Peacock represents success in career, prosperity, beauty, and dignity. In Buddhist tradition the peacock is considered to be Kuan Yin's eyes on the world. The eyes in the feathers were said to have been given to the Peacock to watch over the other animals and keep them from bad behavior.

Fish and other water animals are among the most beloved of creatures. There is a Chinese saying that "Happiness is watching fish" and anyone who has sat near a koi pond or peered into an aquarium can testify to this.

Fish represent freedom, wealth, harmony, and marital bliss. The Chinese character for fish sounds like the word for "abundance" so many Chinese banquets conclude with the presentation of a large fish -a wish for your wealth. In Buddhist tradition, they represent freedom as they can move freely as the unrestrained enlightened being can. They are among the auspicious signs on the footprints of Buddha. Along with other water creatures and birds they are often used in a life-liberating practice of releasing them back to the wild. The practice is said to produce great merit for the people who participate.

Frog symbolizes youth and family members or money that will return. Frogs also represent reclaiming lost opportunities, finding lost money, or having a chance to acquire money. Toads are also a symbol of longevity.

Turtles represent longevity, strength, and endurance. The Turtle or Tortoise is said to conceal the secrets of heaven and earth. Its shell is flat on the bottom like earth and vaulted above like the sky. It was said that the Ba-Gua markings were originally found on the tortoise shell and they are often used in fortune-telling.

Fences, Walls, and other Boundaries

Boundary separations have been around since people began to claim property as their own. There are many ways that you can separate yourself from neighbors. The most common is the wall or fence; however, plants alone can also create the boundary. In the design process, you need to figure out which of the many options you want for a boundary.

Fences and walls range from solid separations to transparent separation. When designing a fence be mindful of the proportions. If the fence is too high in relationship to the house and the size of the lot, you will feel like a prisoner. This can translate to you feeling trapped financially, in an unhappy marriage, or having debilitating health problems.

When I am designing a boundary wall or fence I am also mindful of the way I will integrate it with the entry to the garden. Entries are an important component of any landscape design because you are previewing the energy for the property and providing the main path of ch'i to the house. (I will deal more with entries later in this chapter.)

You can use plants for a fence but stay away from using hibiscus and azalea especially as a continuous planting. Good choices for the plants for boundaries are ones from the bamboo or the pine family. This would give you an edge that symbolizes flexibility, friendship, fidelity, wisdom, and longevity or longevity and strength.

Wood fences offer you many options. There are many companies that produce a beautiful bamboo

This beautifully designed bamboo fence could be improved by painting it green.

fence that will give you all the attributes of Bamboo. Painting it green would be better because the natural way that Bamboo fades appears dead. Another color that isn't good is yellow, which is also considered a dead color. One of the best colors is the black bamboo and even better is purple bamboo which is rare and considered sacred because it is said that Kuan Yin stayed in a forest of purple bamboo.

If you have a fence made of some other wood you might also want to paint it green so that it looks livelier. Many fences age gray. This is fine but not as good as other colors. Red is a good color for a fence. White isn't as favorable and black fences are the worst. If you have a white or black fence you can add plants to screen it and add vitality to it. A black fence can be cured by adding gold to the tips of the fence. When you go to palaces, you often see black fences topped with gold so it represents regal situations.

If you use wrought iron for a fence you need to take care that you don't make it look like you are in jail. If you already have a fence like this, plant vines to soften and hide it or add gold tips to the top for a powerful cure. Other ways to adjust wrought iron fences as well as introduce beauty to your fence is to have patterns woven into them. One beautiful pattern is the golden cicada, symbolic of longevity and resurrection.

Some people like to use less substantial material such as chicken wire or chain link. If you use one of these, plant a vine or hedge around it.

Many of the same ideas apply to solid walls as they do with fences. The colors discussed for fences apply to walls as well. In China one of the most beautiful ways to accentuate a wall is called a dragon wall because its roof tiles on top look like dragon scales. One person put yellow tiles on top of the fence to connote the

Wrought iron with Gold Tips and plants to soften it.

See the Cicada pattern in the fence.

The dragon wall is not only beautiful but adds a sense of movement to the garden.

Lotus, a symbol of purity on the wall

This lattice adds beauty to the plain wall.

Chinese emperor as that color was once the exclusive purview of the Imperial Family. Red, which is thought to be lucky, is often used. Both of these colors are inauspicious with the dragon motif as they are indicative of a cooked dragon. Green, black, or gray would be fine. As if these walls aren't beautiful enough, many times they are punctuated with windows to other parts of the garden in beautiful shapes that add another element of fantasy.

Another way to lend interest and beauty to a wall is to add a lattice or motif at the top of the wall. Here you see two examples, one with a beautiful carved lotus and a contemporary wood lattice above a wall.

Stone walls are excellent for retired people. They are so beautiful and are "rock solid" but would inhibit the career of a working person. It is forbidding and heavy for a person who is still out and engaged in the world.

This entry gate is topped with two dragons playing with a pearl, which represents power and very good luck.

When considering fences, you should also think about entry gates. An arched entry gate is fine as long as it isn't painted gray. Second to gray, white isn't good either. For some guidelines on gates: If you have a gate that leads to the property, it should be bigger and/ or wider than your front door. This is to accentuate the largest entry for good energy to come your way. Using the same principle, if you have a back gate, be sure it isn't larger than the front gate as you don't want good energy to leave quickly. It bears repeating that you want a large welcoming gate to enter to your property.

The rainbow-colored gate shown here is a bold show-stopper.

Many people choose beautiful motifs on their entry gates. The most common ones that I've seen in wrought iron are nonobjective; that is, no particular image that is impressed but rather beautiful scrolled work.

Beautiful flower or leaf images on fences, walls, and gates also promote good energy. Using color or texture on walls, fences, and gates is great. If you really want to emphasize good luck at your entry, you can use red. Vermillion symbolizes wealth and prominence and it also has the effect of warding off evil ch'i and accumulating auspiciousness.

A bit gaudy for some but imaginative and whimsical.

One of the most wonderful experiences I have had with a wall was peeking into this narrow alley to be enchanted with the wall covering. Although this is for a commercial site, there is no reason you can't create a knockout experience like this for yourself.

Paving

Feeling the solid earth under your feet is an important experience. You can use almost any material for paving the front walkway and the rest of the property. The important issues are safety, comfort, beauty, maintenance, and appropriateness to the site, neighborhood, and architecture.

Most Western landscape designs actually deemphasize paving and tend to make it uniform and uninteresting. I took literally hundreds of pictures of paving in China. The workmanship is so beautiful and at every turn there is a different incredible motif. Incorporating one motif

Plum blossoms in black and white express spring and yin-yang balance.

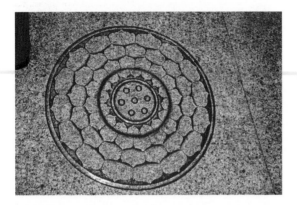

This lotus signals the beginning of a new space.

or another, whether it is a feng shui one or something that is beautiful and sacred to you and your sensibilities, is a wonderful way to greet yourself every day.

I have seen such simple ideas as adding shell pieces in asphalt paving that adds beauty, texture, and meaning to an otherwise uninspired option. In China and various other cultures shells were used for money so using them in paving particularly in the Career area of the property could lead to generating more money through your Career.

Other ideas about improving paving would be to integrate special patterns. One that is seen widely is the plum blossom, symbol of spring and new beginnings. Already referenced is a pattern called cracked ice which also symbolizes the ending of cold, difficult times and the beginning of warmth and new possibilities. An octagon shape integrated into the paving refers to the sacred Ba-Gua and reminds you of the feng shui promise that is in store for you. Many of these patterns employ black and white colored stones to symbolize the balance of yin and yang.

In China an important feature tile or carving in the pavement is often placed in an entry where there is a change of direction or the end of an area. Again, these special notations in the pavement can be anything. There are beautiful deer carvings, lotus symbols, crane mosaics, and dragons impressions, for example.

The image of the Ching Dynasty coins represents the treasury of the wealthiest dynasty in Chinese history. As there were ten rulers of this dynasty who accumulated wealth, the coins struck during their reign represent great abundance and good fortune. I have seen a few alternatives of this motif and have created some wonderful versions of it myself. Sometimes they are represented in a straight line. Other times there are sets flanking both sides of the walkway. Sometimes the coins dance like dragons toward the entry.

Entries Set the Stage

Entries are among the most important parts of the consideration of the landscape because they welcome ch'i to your home. To repeat, the best is to have a big, wide, and tall entry gate. In China you often see what I think of as a crescendo gate. You could also look at it as if it were an arrowhead, taller in the middle and descending on both sides to create a sense of majesty as you enter.

Entries are often protected from evil spirits by Fu Dogs flank-

This crescendo gate gives you a sense of importance when you walk through it.

ing both sides. These protectors are another classic example of yin and yang as the one on the left as you face the building is usually male with the earth controlled under his paw and the one on the right is usually the female with her paw protecting her child.

Next, I have an odd instruction but it comes about because I have seen this situation many times. The walkway should be continuous from the house to the street. Sometimes people build a walkway that ends just short of the street because they don't want to chance losing a portion of the walkway if the city widens the street. I can assure you that much more money was lost in that household by breaking the energy link than would have been lost in building through a city dedication area.

Safety is always paramount with front walkways. My client recently was unhappy with the continuous red brick walkway because the steps had different size risers. Because people don't always perceive the difference, tripping is common with this situation. Unfortunately, in this case I had to advise him to replace the steps and walkway entirely.

I have seen some beautifully done front walkways that are very narrow. If it feels as though you could fall off the path on the way to the door, the path is too narrow. Some houses don't have walkways at all and it is difficult to determine how to get to the front door. This situation isn't as bad as some front yards that look like you will be impaled by cactus or other thorny plants if you dare enter.

Some houses have a hidden entry. If an entry is perpendicular to the street with no view of the front door from the street, it is a hidden entry. I have even seen many cases where there is no visible link from the entry to the street. You could stand at the entry and because there is no strong differentiated walkway you have no clue where to go. On a mundane level, it is important to show your visitors where to enter your house with a strong walkway that is large or has patterned paving or special lighting that leads you to that front door. Transcendentally, it would be good to add a convex mirror across from the front door to pull the ch'i from the street to the front door.

While we are on the subject of entries, let's look at driveways. A driveway that is directed straight to your front door is not good. It would be better to curve the driveway; a curved driveway that starts curving from off the property is very good. If a driveway narrows, place a fountain on both sides half-way up the driveway or alternatively place sculptures on both sides to keep the energy from decreasing as it arrives at your house.

Pools and Ponds

We have mentioned pools and other water features many times. The positive attributes are many as water brings prosperity into our lives. A crescent-shaped gutter, pool, or pond which curves inward toward the main entrance will bring excellent finance, good health, and promising career to the inhabitants. This is another way of bringing the water to the front door.

Whenever I drive by a shopping center that is failing and its water feature is pouring water toward the neighborhood instead of toward the stores I am reminded of an important principle. In the early days before I knew about feng shui I designed a pool where the water poured away from the house. Years later, when teaching my client in one of my classes, I was able to give her the cure of adding a convex mirror over the front door that would draw the money spilling away into the house.

A pool that is too close to the house will overwhelm the house with instability. If you already have this situation, you can add nine pots of plants between the house and the pool or pond to stabilize the energy. The same cure would be used if the pool or pond was so large that it overwhelms the yard. That again would create instability.

The worst situation is when the corner of a pool or pond is pointing at the house. A pond or pool with its sharp tip pointing at the main entrance of a house can bring head illnesses, ocular diseases, eye or ear, and gynecological diseases to the inhabitants of the house. It is just as bad if it is pointing at the master bedroom or kitchen. The cure can either be same nine potted plants around the point or, if it is in the front of the house, you can use a concave mirror over the front door to disperse the negative energy.

It is best not to place a pool in the Fame position because of the conflict of water with the fire element found in Fame. You can alleviate this by placing nine potted plants between the house and pool to support the fire element. This would be one area that I would prefer to see trees or strong shrubs which are considered to be wood elements to support the fire of Fame.

One of the best places for a swimming pool is the Wealth corner. The Relationship corner is good as well. Remember if you have a spa that spills water or fountains around the pool that the water pours toward the house, not away from it.

If the swimming pool is inside the lock of the shape of the house, be careful about the safety of swimmers. The lock shape is when two parts of the house extend out and the pool is in the middle of the two extensions. The cure is to use nine pots of plants protecting the U indentation. This cure offers enough vitality to bring safety with it

Seating in the Garden

Seating in the garden should be comfortable and safe. I like to create several places in the garden to rest, reflect, and enjoy a different view. What aspects are important for seating? A physically comfortable seat is important. A metal bench in either freezing weather or scorching sun is uncomfortable. Wood, while comfortable, needs to be maintained and if maintenance isn't proper, you could have splinters that will be embarrassing to remove.

A seating area that is unprotected doesn't feel safe. If you place a bench in the middle of the yard with nothing behind you and nothing overhead, you will feel like you are in a fishbowl. Without a tree or an overhead structure to shade you, you may not feel at ease sitting in the garden. I like to place seating in corners or at the edges where you can get a vista of the garden or a spectacular part of the garden.

A Potpourri of Other Elements

Including a greenhouse is very positive as it will add to the greenery and vitality of your home. One caution is to immediately repair broken glass because broken glass can affect your eyes and your reputation.

A tennis court is best if it is in the back of the property, in the Wealth, Fame, or Relationship areas. It is not good in the front of the property, in the Knowledge, Career, or Helpful People areas. Upkeep for the tennis court should not exceed one-third of the owner's income. If a tennis court is too expensive, you become a slave to it so that instead of being a joy and good recreation, it drags your energy down.

Children's play areas are best located in the Family, Relationship, or Children's part of the property or yard. The best colors for play equipment are original wood, sky blue, or green.

Garbage or compost is best placed in Relationship position. This symbolizes earth and everything that returns to earth.

Many parts of the landscape are unseen but still crucial to the feng shui of the property. We never see the irrigation system unless it breaks. Make sure that there are no blockages or leaks in the irrigation heads. If those arise, fix them immediately. Long-term neglect of issues could lead to excretory or nerve problems.

A septic tank facing your front door or in the Fame area of your property will negatively affect your feng shui. To cure the problem, place a potted plant on top of the lid of the septic tank. The plant should be lush and flourishing. It would be better if the plant had flowers and fruit. As with all cures, remember to perform the Three Secret Reinforcement ceremony with this cure. This cure could be enhanced if you added cinnabar rice in and around the planted pot. (Instructions for preparing cinnabar rice are included in the ceremony chapter).

A septic tank in the Wealth or the Relationship area of the lot needs no cure, though you can do it if you want to. In this location it symbolizes that the fertilizer of the septic system will feed the plants and helps your family to grow stronger so it is advantageous to add the cure.

Propane tanks outside the house are generally unattractive. You can paint them green or hide them with a plant or other screen. If you have a propane tank underground, place flower pots on top with of it with cinnabar rice in the pots.

If you have a water tank on your property, paint it green if it is a single shape. If it has four feet on it, paint the feet brown, body green, and then nine red circles indicating fruit on top. You are then simulating a tree with fruit on it. This will be a powerful cure.

If you are designing a sewage system that must drain from the front of the house to the street, add a loop along the sewage line that goes back toward the house. It is best if your sewage system drains from the back of the property. If you already have a sewer that leaves in a straight line to the front of your lot you can do a ceremony with cinnabar rice, dropping it along the ideal sewer route just described.

Make sure all the drainage on the property works properly. Remember that water stuck on the property relates to money being stuck in your life. An off-property drain issue to look for is the street drain location. I had a client who had huge openings for the street drainage all across the front of the property. Money and luck were draining away before they could get to the property. The cure was to add up lighting across the front of the property to pull the ch'i up.

Lighting can do wonders for lifting the energy of the property. We have already discussed cures using lighting when the property is declining in the back and to fill in missing areas, but also pay attention to night lighting throughout the property. Properties should have adequate lighting to see throughout the paths at night, especially at the entry.

There comes a time in every design when you have to take what you have learned and start the planning in earnest. Even for experienced designers this can be uncomfortable. My mentor was a brilliant designer who always told me that the problem for him was narrowing the design decisions. Yet before he began to draw he would go through what I called the design dance. He would walk by the survey drawing sitting on his desk and declare that he didn't have a thought in his head. Next he would pass the drawing again and wonder aloud what the client could have been thinking to hire him. The next time he passed his desk he would say how ugly the site was and that the client wouldn't appreciate what was being done for him anyway. Then of course he would sit down and design a brilliant or several brilliant options for the landscape. Let's see the process in several examples in the next chapter.

Chapter 8

Designing Landscapes with Feng Shui

When designing a landscape we have a clean slate and many choices! Good design always begins with an idea, hope, dream, or vision. The vision is what brings the various divergent areas, elements, or enhancements together. The vision is what makes your landscape a personal statement and an intimate connection to your land.

With vision in hand, the next task is to piece together the elements and materials to be used in the landscape. For a landscape designer or a plant nut, finding the resolve to limit the choices is challenging. For a novice to the landscape world, the task is to learn how to structure the design. A feng shui approach to landscape design can help in both situations. The structure outlined in a feng shui designed garden can help the expert make optimal choices and the novice create the structure for the garden. This chapter will use examples to demonstrate the methods of design, choices, and solutions.

Beginning the Design

In previous chapters we saw how to assemble information. We need to gather a survey, look at the land, the house, the neighborhood, and our needs for the property. Before beginning design, it is important to assess what areas we want to improve in our lives. This aspect of design is one of the ways feng shui landscape design is unique. Determining what is lacking in your life can help prioritize and even set a theme for the landscape design. This theme can be set for the entire property or can be established for each separate part of the property. With the goals set, and the property evaluated, we are ready to begin to map out the landscape design. Through examples, this chapter will show you how this all takes place.

Image, Intention, Action: Three Ways to Avoid Change

Most of us want to change our lives for the better. Yet I have seen many clients not take the very action that will help to support or create the change. Changing one's life and fortune can be a fearful process. I have seen clients exhibit this fear in three ways. Some people cannot build a new image for themselves. When they think about changing their lives, they can't imagine anything better for themselves or they limit how much life can improve. Other people will not claim the personal power or intention to bring about a change. Lastly, some people who fear change become paralyzed and won't take action. Identifying the place that you get stuck is the first step to facing the fear and changing the pattern.

When you have a clear image about the things you want for your life, it is more likely the forces will come together to produce the desired results. This is why it is important to identify the areas that you want to improve and the exact improvements you want to see. Many of my clients have looked at the visualization part of the process as an extension to goal setting in their lives. This is not the best way of viewing it because many of us are fearful of setting aims that we might not meet. An alternative way is to visualize the most expansive ideal of your future. Everything begins as an image and image always precedes matter. In other words, the images of today become the realities of tomorrow.

Many of us have dreams about our desires but not the sense of personal power to manifest our dreams. Intention, making a decision to change, is the bridge that moves an image into action. The drives behind our intentions are as diverse as the number of people who hold them. Some people need a big picture important life mission to fuel their intentions. When I hear people use words like "hope" and "try," it is a signal that they aren't going to fuel their action with intention and are setting themselves up to fail.

Sometimes people get stuck in the action phase. They have the plans and the intention but don't implement even simple changes. This is usually due to fear of failure or fear of change. Some people have been conditioned to think of change as something that is foisted upon them which is often difficult and painful. At one time in my life I felt that way as well but after I spent some time in self-reflection, I realized that whenever change came about, its end result was to my benefit. In fact, when I had foresight of the change, it could have been smoother had I embraced and initiated it myself.

We need to face our fears of change so that we are willing to create images that fuel our intentions to embrace a better future through our action. All three parts are necessary in order to create positive change in our lives.

What We Want and What We Have

Analyzing our property begins with evaluating what we want and what we have. To begin the evaluation, review Applying Feng Shui to your Property in Chapter 5. After assessing your needs and analyzing the property, the next step is connecting with the land. This can take the form of sitting quietly or meditating on the land with the intention of getting additional information. Here we are looking for concepts or details of the design and how it melds with the property and the house. When I am doing this for myself, this most often happens when I am weeding, trimming, or fertilizing. For a client, sometimes this happens when I am taking additional measurements, putting the property on my computer to analyze it, or just looking at pictures of the property. Between the analysis, your needs, and communing with the land, a concept or image or theme for the property is born. Let's see how this process comes together.

Example One: A Home on Flat Land

This home is on a beautiful tree-lined street in California. The backyard was totally concrete except for a planter with a tree, a fountain and a wood deck and Jacuzzi in the Wealth corner. Heavy overhead structures shaded the Fame and Relationship areas making them dark and uninviting. There was no garage. The rear yard faces south so it is a very hot space.

There is a high degree of indoor/outdoor interface. There are many windows and doors on both the front and back side of the house that face the garden. This made the views from the house particularly important. They like privacy from the street but wanted visual access to the street.

There are no negative neighborhood conditions.

The previous owners of the property all loved the house, had raised families and prospered there.

The lot is perfectly rectangular and consequently has no missing parts and no extensions. The house configuration has missing parts in Career and Helpful People. There are extensions in the Helpful People and Wealth areas. The house is entered through the Career and Knowledge areas.

The Client's Image

The husband wanted to be greeted with an exciting, colorful landscape in a front yard that wasn't too different from the neighborhood. He needed a garage to tinker in. He wanted a yard that he could stroll through and an area to practice golf. The wife wanted to create a spiritual experience for the family. She is a gardener and loves a variety of plants, a space for meditation, and surprises around the property.

Both husband and wife have favorite colors and fragrances. He loves honeysuckle, night-blooming jasmine and bright, hot colors. She loves jasmine, lavender, lilac, roses, and herbs and the cool colors, purple, white, and black. (Notice how he chose the yang colors and she chose the yin colors.) They both like a casual informal garden look.

The Client's Intention

Both husband and wife wanted to improve all areas of their life but especially their Career, Wealth, and Fame. The client was very willing to put the plan into action but procrastinated at various junctures to give them time to acclimate to the changes and to see how their lives would change correspondingly. Once they were truly ready to embrace the potential shifts that could occur, construction began.

Into Action

The action began by removing all the concrete and the overhead structures in the rear yard and building an attractive garage structure. Here we bump up against the realities of working with feng shui. The best and logical place to put the garage is in the Relationship corner; however, in terms of feng shui that can cause the marriage to come apart. The client believes in feng shui but must have the garage. The solution to this is to do a powerful transcendental cure (to be discussed later) to alleviate the issue. Next, a rock-lined waterfall/fishpond was built that is partially in the Career area in an embracing shape to bring the beneficial effects of the water toward the front door. A Buddha was placed at the top honor position of the pond. As the entry is set back from the street and because of the wall not clearly visible, several sets of wind chimes were placed from the entry gate to the front door of the house. Planting around the property was designed primarily in the Ba-Gua colors with balancing elements in each area. The fountain in the rear yard was put into working order. Over time some aspects of the property changed. As the initial expenses were substantial, the putting green wasn't added until years later.

The Plan

In Ill. 8-1 see the existing conditions of the plan and how the Ba-Gua overlays on the property. The majority of the front yard is in the Knowledge, Career, and Helpful People areas. The entire rear yard except for the covered porch is in the Wealth, Fame, and Relationship areas. The property naturally lends itself to the creation of at least three separate spaces. The area in front of the wall on the street side is a public space for the enjoyment of the neighborhood and the first greeting of the clients and guests. The entry courtyard is the beginning of the private space of the property, and the purpose of this space offered the client a separation signaling that they have arrived home. The rear yard is to be a lively working space for the pleasure of the four rooms that face onto the space.

In Ill. 8-2 you see the Ba-Gua applied to the home and to the office. Notice that the home is oriented in the same direction as the property while the office is oriented in a different direction. The house has no "problem" or missing areas, and in fact has extensions in Helpful People, Knowledge, and Wealth; however, the office has a missing Helpful People corner that must be fixed.

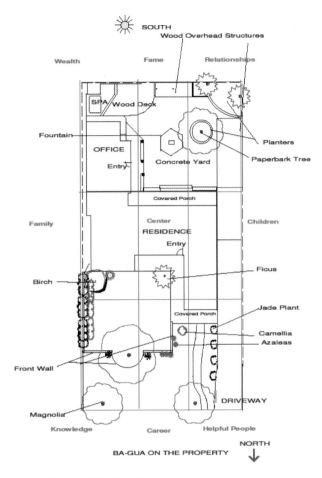

Ill. 8-1 The Ba-Gua on existing property

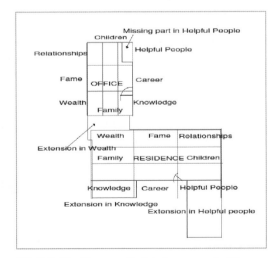

Ill. 8-2 Ba-Gua applied to home and office

123

Explaining the Plan

Because the property is broken into three distinct areas, each space will be discussed separately. The ch'i on the property has no major blockages. In the rear of the property, there was some lack of life force due to the preponderance of concrete but with the reestablishment of a planted yard, that issue would be resolved. The yin-yang balance is pretty good on the property. The rear south-facing yard is too yang, especially in the summer. With additional plants and the existing fountain, the ambient temperature, glare, and heat will be reduced. The addition of the garage removed two shrubs that were a natural cure to the telephone pole in that area; however, the garage and Paperbark Tree as well as offsite trees have obliterated the effect of the pole on the property. The front of the property is well balanced. There are no large trees confronting (directly in front of) the front door and when you view the plan you can see that in fact there are trees that are almost all the way around the house, which is very auspicious.

The five elements are represented throughout the property. The walkways and curved front wall represent the water shape. The mature trees and the green plants represent Wood both in front and back. Fire is abundant in the red tile and brick walkways and porches. The wall material, the paving material, and the flat shape of the house roof represent Earth. Metal is represented by the white house trim and the metal light fixtures throughout the property. In summary, there are minimal adjustments that needed to be made as a result of the existing ch'i on the property.

Street Yard Plan

The street yard area falls in the Knowledge, Career, and Helpful People areas of the property. The clients wanted a lawn to harmonize with the neighborhood. Because the wall is such a distinct and pleasant shape, it was mirrored in the lawn. The shape of the lawn conveys a movement and flow like the water element which represents the Career area. The Knowledge area was originally planted with primarily blue plants such as Australian

Bluebell Creeper and Blue Hibiscus for height and the silhouette it creates against the wall. Unfortunately, because the light was tricky there, the Blue Hibiscus had to be replaced with the Tree Mallow. The Tree Mallow was chosen for its pink flowers because the Knowledge

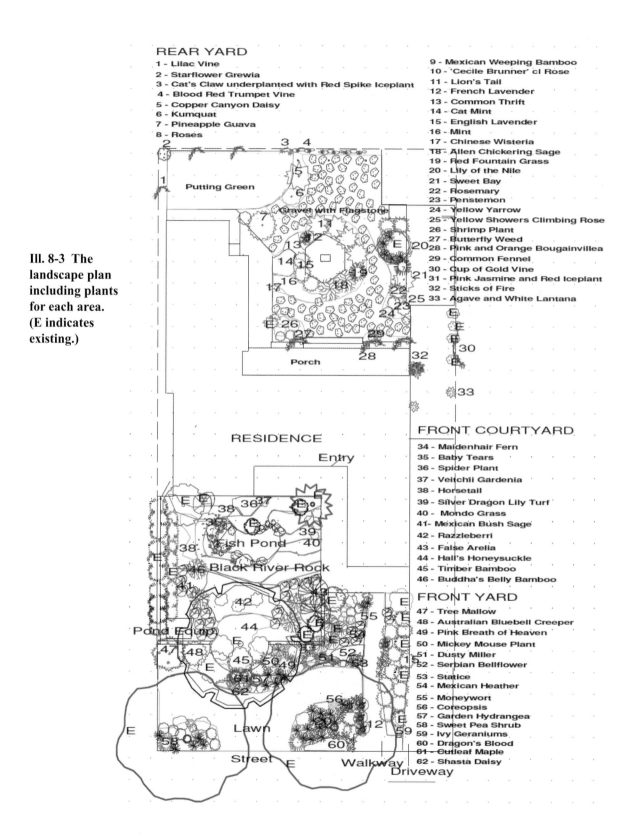

REAR YARD
1 - Lilac Vine
2 - Starflower Grewia
3 - Cat's Claw underplanted with Red Spike Iceplant
4 - Blood Red Trumpet Vine
5 - Copper Canyon Daisy
6 - Kumquat
7 - Pineapple Guava
8 - Roses
9 - Mexican Weeping Bamboo
10 - 'Cecile Brunner' cl Rose
11 - Lion's Tail
12 - French Lavender
13 - Common Thrift
14 - Cat Mint
15 - English Lavender
16 - Mint
17 - Chinese Wisteria
18 - Allen Chickering Sage
19 - Red Fountain Grass
20 - Lily of the Nile
21 - Sweet Bay
22 - Rosemary
23 - Penstemon
24 - Yellow Yarrow
25 - Yellow Showers Climbing Rose
26 - Shrimp Plant
27 - Butterfly Weed
28 - Pink and Orange Bougainvillea
29 - Common Fennel
30 - Cup of Gold Vine
31 - Pink Jasmine and Red Iceplant
32 - Sticks of Fire
33 - Agave and White Lantana

Ill. 8-3 The landscape plan including plants for each area. (E indicates existing.)

Putting Green

Gravel with Flagstone

Porch

RESIDENCE

Entry

FRONT COURTYARD
34 - Maidenhair Fern
35 - Baby Tears
36 - Spider Plant
37 - Veitchii Gardenia
38 - Horsetail
39 - Silver Dragon Lily Turf
40 - Mondo Grass
41 - Mexican Bush Sage
42 - Razzleberri
43 - False Arelia
44 - Hall's Honeysuckle
45 - Timber Bamboo
46 - Buddha's Belly Bamboo

Fish Pond

Black River Rock

Pond Equip

FRONT YARD
47 - Tree Mallow
48 - Australian Bluebell Creeper
49 - Pink Breath of Heaven
50 - Mickey Mouse Plant
51 - Dusty Miller
52 - Serbian Bellflower
53 - Statice
54 - Mexican Heather
55 - Moneywort
56 - Coreopsis
57 - Garden Hydrangea
58 - Sweet Pea Shrub
59 - Ivy Geraniums
60 - Dragon's Blood
61 - Cutleaf Maple
62 - Shasta Daisy

Lawn

Street

Walkway

Driveway

Gua is across from and related to the Relationship Gua, and having both colors here is really beneficial. Other blues like Lily of the Nile were also added into the mix. As the landscape developed, Autumn Sage was planted to add yang and fall color for this. The Mickey Mouse Bush with its black berries represents the color for the career. In the foreground is Shasta Daisy, the metal color which feeds water. There were several existing winter flowering azalea background plants. Winter is the season of the water element. The Helpful People area, which has the front walkway running through it, is planted with many gray plants. Three different varieties of Lavender and Statice represent the color for the Helpful People area while the Mexican Heather brings the purple Wealth color into the Helpful People area. At the front of the walkway, Ivy Geranium, one of the protective colorful plants, is used. Near the house was an existing Jade Plant which was retained as it is a good fortune plant.

It was most important to open the narrow entry at the street edge of the walkway so that more good ch'i could enter. Initially this was not implemented due to budget constrictions, and a temporary but effective alternative was employed. The clients used stepping stones set in the dirt to widen the mouth of ch'i. After time, they were able to permanently widen the walkway and in the process embedded Chinese coins from the Ching Dynasty in the mortar at the entrance of the walk.

Though the plants in the front area were selected primarily for their colors and the client's affection for them, the meanings convey welcoming messages. Plants not listed on the plan such as Camellia and Cypress were existing.

Azalea- love, moderation
Chrysanthemum- longevity, joy
Cypress- protection
Hydrangea- love, gratitude
Lavender- devotion, luck, success

Camellia- excellence, beauty
Coreopsis- always cheerful
Gardenia- purity, peace
Ivy Geraniums- protection
Maple Tree- success, balance

Front Courtyard

The first thing that greets you as you enter the front courtyard is the beautiful wind chime that serves to direct energy around the house extension in the Helpful People area. The biggest and most prominent feature of this area is a Shamel Ash, which stands as protector and supporter of the property. The other trees found here are a Birch and a Ficus.

The next sight is the major feature in the front courtyard, the waterfall and fishpond. It is a beautiful, melodious, interesting highlight that greets the owners every day. It can be heard in many parts of the house and provides a sense of harmony and delight for everyone. The Buddha that is ringed by a curtain of green horsetail and backed by Mexican bamboo sets a spiritual theme for the entry.

The entry courtyard includes four areas of the property Ba-Gua, Knowledge, Career, Family, and center. The courtyard is entered through the Career Gua of the property. Like the house and the office, this courtyard could be also examined in terms of a complete Ba-Gua for this space separately as well as the areas represented by the entire property. This discussion will treat this area as the Ba-Gua of the entire property.

Plants that are used to represent the black color Career in this area are the "Black Knight" variety of the butterfly bush and almost black-leaved Elegant Aralia. With the waterfall, the sense of hearing is piqued in this water Gua. The other representatives of water are the dark gray rocks used around the water feature and the dark gray stepping stones that lead close to the water feature and

around the yard for viewing. Also found here is the winter flowering Chinese Fringe Flower.

A blue flowering Australian Bluebell Creeper seen over the wall represents the color of the Knowledge area. Buddha's Belly Bamboo brings a more spiritual aspect to bamboo, whose strength and resilience is supportive in spiritual quests. A Quartz Crystal rock, which is used to attain knowledge, is used around the water feature in this area of the Gua.

The Family area (wood) is represented by the green Horsetail Reeds, Mexican Bamboo, Fern Pine, and Wheeler's Pittosporum. All of these plants are non-flowering evergreen plants. The shape of the Horsetail Reeds and Bamboo are the "wood" shape, tall and columnar. Though there is little color in the family corner the textures play counterpoint to each other. The Buddha here represents the connection to the owner's spiritual lineage.

A small area near the front entry is in the Center area, which represents the Earth element. The largest rock around the water feature in this area was placed horizontally. Atop the rock is another protector of the property, a dragon. Touch is the sense associated with earth and there are several different grasses that create a subtle contrast of textures. Mondo Grass, Lily Turf, and Silver Dragon Lily Turf offer an array of colors and textures that play well against each other. A metal crane sculpture wades through the Lily Turf to support longevity for the owners.

The shapes for the groundcover patterns and the pond/waterfall are designed to reflect the wall shape and provide a relaxed, informal feeling to greet the owners and guests. Gardenias are located close to the porch to provide a much beloved fragrance. A fanciful butterfly-shaped metal bench offers a perch from which this quiet spot can be enjoyed. Near the front door is another wind chime that serves to attract good ch'i to the entry and to call out the owner's message to the world.

There are nine bamboo in the front yard arranged in a shape that embraces the house. Just like a street that supports a house this symbol of friendship, flexibility, brings abundance to the owners.

Along the front driveway there is a white fence that runs from Helpful People through the Children area. This fence has a beautiful mural with lotus, sunflowers, butterflies, poppies, and bees to minimize the amount of white color close to the house.

Meanings of the Front Courtyard Plantings

The front courtyard plants offer more beautiful sentiments for the owners of the house.

Ash Tree- higher awareness
Birch Tree- strength, purity
Fern- fascination
Honeysuckle- bonds of love
Myrtle- love, joy

Bamboo- friendship, support, peace
Butterfly Bush- impetuosity
Gardenia- purity, peace
Mexican Bush Sage- eloquence

The Rear Yard Garden

The rear yard is the most informal garden space on the property. It falls in the Wealth, Fame, and Relationship areas of the property. The rear porch is in the Family, Center, and Children areas. In the rear yard, the husband wanted space for entertaining, roaming, and practicing golf. The wife wanted to have a bright, happy backyard that was inspired from every view.

The rear porch, though small, is important because it is adjacent to the kitchen, dining room, and master bedroom and serves as a launching pad into the yard. The Family area of the porch is outside the master bedroom. A blank wall in an alcove offered an opportunity to design an intimate, interesting area with a small fountain surrounded by green plants. The center area of the porch was left open to allow for French doors to open and friends to spill out into the yard. In this area, two spectacular orange bougainvillea climb up the posts and along the railing. In the Children's area a forged metal bell sounds deep tones with the wind. Outside the kitchen window are hummingbird feeders that delight the owner while washing dishes. An intimate round table and chairs are used for breakfast and quiet dinners in warm weather.

The driveway leading to the rear yard is in the Children's area also. Plants in this area include roses and the Yellow Pot of Gold Vine. Pots in this area include yellow flowering plants such as Poinciana, which represents the earth element supporting the metal element of the Children's area. There are also White Geraniums and fragrant white Lantana used as fillers.

The driveway leads to the Relationship area where the garage was built. Roses, the flower of love, flank the garage and a large Bay Laurel, Paperbark Tree, and Rosemary hide most of the garage from the house. Because the Paperbark Tree was existing on the property, the owners made accommodations to keep it by limiting the size of the garage so that it could remain. The Bay Laurel is very appropriate in the Relationship Gua, as in Greek legends it is associated with passionate love. Its meaning of wisdom connects it closely to the Knowledge area across the Ba-Gua. The blue flowered Rosemary also connects it to Knowledge while its meaning of fidelity makes it perfect for the Relationship area.

The Fame area has an orange painted wood structure with a gold sun sculpture on it. What better to represent the fire element? Under the sun is the orange flowering Copper Canyon Daisy. It is in the Marigold family and so gives a wonderful fragrance when you brush up against it. In the same area a Kumquat Tree offers its orange fruits up in time for Chinese New Year's good luck and adds the taste element to the Fame/Fire area. Over the wood structure is the red flowering Blood Red Trumpet Vine.

A Pineapple Guava Tree fills the missing corner of the Helpful People office area. A wind chime was added to the entry of the office to attract ch'i to this space.

The majority of the lot's Wealth area is filled by the office and golf putting green. This is appropriate here as most people think of golf as an upper echelon activity. To use the space at night there is plenty of strong light which also helps to lift the ch'i. Planting space around the green is filled with Lilac Vine, Starflower Grewia, and Purple Trumpet Vine, all purple flowering plants.

Plant Meanings for the Rear Yard

The rear yard is the place where the family spends the most time so the plants are most important here.

Bay Leaf- wisdom, acquired & innate
Kumquat Tree- gold good fortune
Rose- love, beauty
Sage- esteem

Cat Mint- Ivy Geraniums - protection
Marigold- passion and creativity
Rosemary- fidelity
Wisteria- welcome

Results of the Changes

Several years have passed since the landscape has been installed. Both husband and wife have seen major changes in every area of their lives. Both have had shifts in their careers that have been welcome surprises. They are receiving help from previously unknown sources and they have both learned what was needed to move them forward on their life paths. Both members of the couple have never felt more creative and this is demonstrated in their work. Their passionate relationship has remained unchanged and relationships with clients have blossomed into many new friendships. Both members of the couple have found the most change in the areas of Fame and Wealth. As a result of the rise of their reputations, they have both received more business and better revenues. The husband's business has increased 20 percent and the wife's business has doubled!!

While all of this sounds idyllic, remember that the changes came as the result of their image, intention, and action. As these areas have shifted, they have come to see that other imbalances have occurred. They can use more peace and relaxation and more attention in the health area. Change always offers the opportunity for new images, new intentions, and new action. They will be adjusting the health area with some stones to provide stability and new positive understanding for the next step.

Example Two: Converting a Home to a Corporation

This house was purchased for the purpose of having a corporate office close to the existing furniture store. The lot is on a corner. The lot is a complete rectangular shape. As you can see, we orient the lot beginning at the driveway entrance. There is nothing particularly notable about the lot that needs correction except that along the Wealth, Fame, and Relationship side, there is a large apartment building that looms over the house.

When you examine the Ba-Gua of the house you see that the front door is in the Career area and there are extensions in Helpful People, Knowledge, and Relationship areas. There is

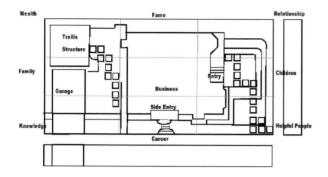

Ill. 8-4 The Ba-Gua on the lot

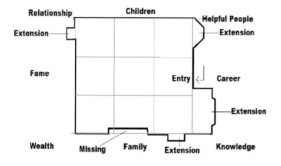

Ill. 8-5 The Ba-Gua on the house shows missing areas.

a missing area in the Family area where a side door enters the house. The missing area will need to be adjusted to gain all of the support that is needed for success.

The client never uses the front door but enters the building through a side door. Because the energy for a space always begins at the front door he was advised to use it weekly at a minimum. The design will include a method to make that more attractive.

The Client's Image and Intention

The client was beginning a new phase of his business. He began by reselling antique furniture and the vision for his business was expanded to designing furniture and selling internationally. He wanted to enhance the reputation and visibility for himself and his company.

The client's aesthetic vision was to have an understated landscape with an Asian flavor. He was committed to a feng shui approach to the landscape and being a designer himself meant that he was eager to be involved in all of the design decisions.

The Plan

The first part of a plan is establishing the vision. Because the client wants a worldwide influence and expansion, we decided to start with the concept of water. The water element has to do with wisdom and social interaction. It is an expanding element. My first concept involved a pool or pond near the front door. The client didn't want the maintenance required for a pond so we settled on a conceptual pond using black river rock. At the entry I wanted to capture the traffic from both streets and funnel it into the Career so I designed a "walkway" that started at the corner, with a very wide profile which meandered to the front door. To conserve costs we decided to use concrete pavers for the walkway. Aesthetically, I love the look of the pavers with grass in between; however, this is not my favorite solution because of the feng shui implications. Though your eye completes the path, the fact that there is material between the pavers like grass and bark breaks the continuous line of energy.

We selected a Purple Plum tree as a focal point walking up the front walkway. As a foundation plant around the building we settled on Horsetail,

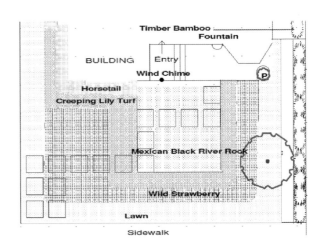

Ill. 8-6 The front area shows the change in textures to the front door.

which has a bamboo look to it and has a strong upward growth pattern. In the front of the building we added layers for texture and interest. The layer below Horsetail is Creeping Lily Turf and flat to the ground is Wild Strawberry. The increase in height from Mexican Black pebbles to Creeping Lily Turf and then decrease to Wild Strawberry and finally to Lawn represents a wave that will extend the influence of the company far and wide. In this composition the plants don't flower but vary in heights and textures.

Finally, we added a wall fountain at the entry. This will take a minimum of maintenance for the owner and the wind chime at the entry calls attention to the major mouth of ch'i for the house.

Along the side of the house where the client and the staff usually enter the building, we designed a larger entry so the mouth of ch'i

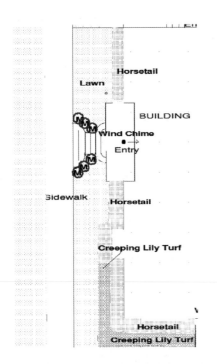

Ill. 8-7 The side entry to the office

is larger at the sidewalk to invite more good energy in. This entry is in the Career area of the lot Ba-Gua. To acknowledge this area and to further accentuate the entry, we added the Dwarf

True Myrtle. We also added another wind chime on the porch near the missing Family area to fill in and complete the area.

The backyard was designed as a space where the employees could enjoy their breaks and lunch with relief from the sun in a pleasurable environment. It was also designed to entertain clients and subcontractors. The motif continued from the front to the back. The materials used in the front of the property were used in the rear as well. Pavers lead from the back door of the building through the lawn pools to the pond metaphor in the Wealth corner of the lot. There was an existing trellis structure but prior to adding the stepping stones leading here, it seemed like a leftover area behind the garage. Giving style and shape to the lawn added interest to the look in the backyard and the textures and heights of groundcover also provide interest. The Timber Bamboo continues around the edge of the property providing privacy from the apartment building. A fountain was added to the lawn outside the Wealth corner of the building so that the sound of water permeates both the Wealth corner of the lot and the office. The Wealth corner of the lot has black Mexican river rock, again to recall water in the Wealth corner.

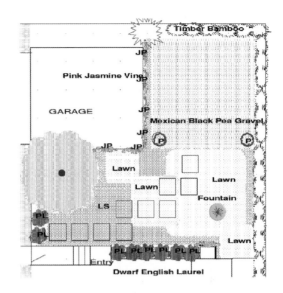

Ill. 8-8   The rear yard is an oasis.

After the Installation

Not all of the recommendations were installed. Despite that, after the installation the company expanded dramatically. Within two years they were given special recognition from an organization of potential clients. Their business has expanded from local to nationwide to worldwide. Within several years they moved to a more corporate setting and continue to innovate and provide beauty to the world.

Example Three: Home on a Hill

The house is set on an eight acre lot overlooking a beautiful agricultural valley. The lot slopes sharply up from the street so that the house is over sixty feet above the street. This is an ideal feng shui position for the house and office. The position is a command position, sitting above the street and protected by the hill in the rear. It is in the front third of the lot, which isn't as good as being in the middle of the lot. This gives it more exposure to the whims of the world. The conditions of the lot are:

The street is on a slope and curves away from the house, which means that the owners may not be able to hold onto the good luck that comes their way.

There are no negative neighborhood conditions.

There is no negative predecessor energy.

A long curving concrete driveway connects the house to the street.

At the street edge is a white corral fence that extends up the driveway on the lower side of the driveway. Retaining walls are on the upper side of the driveway.

The lot has many pine trees lining the driveway and an assortment of other trees. The client wants to create a lush environment planted with many more trees.

The slopes leading up to the house are bare except for the trees planted on them.

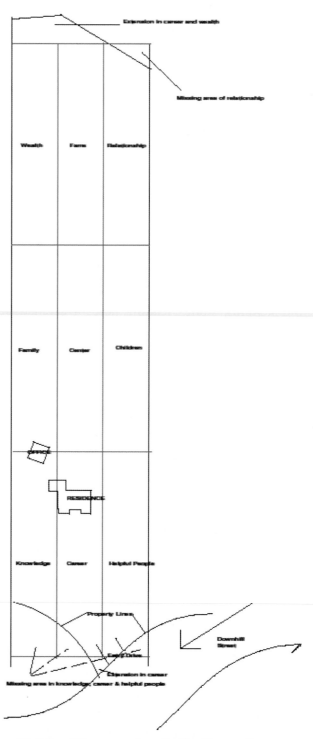

Ill. 8-9   When you place the Ba-Gua on the property you see missing areas and a street problem.

134

A flat pad contains the house, garage, a recently converted office, pool, gazebo, tennis court and reptile areas.

The entry, house and all of the landscape areas to be designed are in the Knowledge, Career. and Helpful People areas of the lot. The rest of the lot is uphill and unused. The clients intend to develop the upper parts of the lot at a future time.

The clients live in a house on the property and run the husband's consulting firm from an office recently added. The client's son is in charge of setting the objectives and securing the construction of the landscape.

The Client's Image and Intention

The image for the landscape were as follows:

Diverse- many types of plants, like a botanical garden
Different- landscape with a flair.
Lush- "Take me away from the desert"
Mystery- "Wow, what's next?" "I didn't expect that."
Color- As many different as possible
East- Asian Influence
Organic- Not structured, but flowing like an organic sculpture
Texture- Play with textures everywhere.
Attraction- "I want bees, birds, hummingbirds, lizards, etc. I want the garden to be a feast for nature and a feast for the senses!"
Smell- As many distinctly different smells as possible. They say the sense of smell is the most powerful when it comes to memories. I want this garden to be a portal to the past, present, and future!

The client runs a consulting business from an office on the property that employs members of the family. It is the intention that the business grows, prospers, and expands. They would like consistency in their financial flow. They have excellent relationships with family members and want improved business relationships.

The son wants an expressive landscape where he can meditate and find meaning in watching a luxurious environment evolve.

The Plan

The primary feng shui challenges are to "cure": 1. The difficult relationship with the street pulling away from the house (which is augmented by the grade of the downhill slope of the street). 2. Filling in the missing areas in Knowledge and Relationship. 3. Improving the energy from the street to the house. 4. Fixing the missing areas of the house and the office.

Once the energy is in the motor court between the house and the office, directing the energy to the "hidden entry" at the front door is the second order of importance. Meeting the client's aesthetic requests is the third most important issue. If energy is not delivered to the office and residence, all other issues become secondary because the household will not be prosperous and healthy.

Yang energy dominates this location. The slope of the land is yang; the hot sun is almost inescapable; the glare from concrete, walls, and the office increases the heat. Trees that were planted by the owner have helped to create shade but more needs to be added to create balance.

Both the house and the office have a classic Chinese lock shape. In the case of the house, no important room such the kitchen is in front of the entry door. The office has already compensated for the missing area with a round planter and a fountain in to pull the entry forward. The front door to the house is blocked and hidden by plant material. At the front door, an overhang creates a dark space and the existing palms are too sharp for this small space.

Explaining the Plan

Often when formulating a theme for a property, an idea presents itself and demands attention but is unworkable in its initial form. So it was with the theme for this property. While meditating on the property, I had a strong sense that there needed to be a stream running from the house to the street. This would provide a metaphor for connecting to the stream of life and partaking of the abundance that the stream has to offer. A recirculating stream over the expanse between the house and the street would necessitate a pool being built at the entry to recirculate and then "catch" the energy. Because the cost would be prohibitive this idea was discarded. A variation of that idea would be a dry streambed to connect the house and office to the street. In terms of feng shui, though, this would represent energy moving downhill away from the house, negating any of the benefits of adding the earth element of rocks and the connection to the street. So a third idea was born, using the resemblance of a stream in shape with color to move the energy uphill. This became the workable solution.

There are certain sequences of color that are naturally seen as rising. The sequence of colors in a rainbow begins with red at the lowest frequency of the spectrum and rises to orange, yellow, green, blue, indigo, and purple. Using this information, the "stream" is created beginning with red at the street juncture and rising through the spectrum to purple at the house and office areas. The stream is built on the visible (upside) of the driveway and mirrored in vines along the fence on the lower side of the driveway.

With the major energy adjustment solved, all of the other parts of the design are orchestrated around the property. Some of the ch'i solutions dovetail into the stream such as drawing energy up to the front door. Continuing the color stream toward the entry did this. Energy was then captured in a waterfall and pond feature that circulates near the door. Some other design elements are not directly related to the stream but recall the prominent concepts.

For ease of discussion, the plan will be discussed in four areas seen in Ill. 8-10. Area 1 includes the entry area. Area 2 includes much of the space visible from the entry and a meditation area. Area 3 includes the upper slope and the areas contiguous to the house. Area 4 is the area around the motor court, entry to the front door, and the area surrounding the office.

Each property offers the

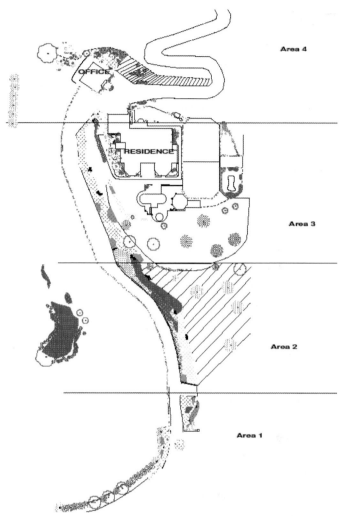

Ill. 8-10 The property divided into four areas

opportunity to combine all of the knowledge and tools of the trade together in a new and unique package. Because the client was open to all possibilities, this project offered the opportunity to use meaningful shapes and plants throughout the design. Though the client wanted "lush," which translates to "water thirsty" in plant connoisseur's vocabulary, most of the plants were selected for their hardiness and drought tolerance to acknowledge the climatic condition of the land and the knowledge that this large piece of property would require plants that largely maintain themselves. Otherwise, each plant chosen was included to fulfill the theme and the descriptions provided by the client.

Area 1 - Entering the Property

The client request along the street side of the property was that the horse corral near the street be screened from view and that the entry be a welcoming experience.

The feng shui goals for the entry were:

To attract auspicious ch'i into the property.

Block the downhill street pressure from the upward side of the street.

Fill in the missing area in the Knowledge Career, and Helpful People Guas.

The solutions for the goals begin with the use of red, which is employed to draw ch'i to the entry. In the color planting scheme here, red is a dominant feature for its dual ability to attract favorable ch'i and to begin the rainbow color scheme. Grevillea "Firespite," which has striking red year-round flowers and lures birds, is used to screen the corral fence. An existing California pepper tree at the southwest corner of the property together with the red-colored plants are uplifting elements. The tree is also used to fill in the missing part of the Gua.

At the entry driveway, several trees that were crowding the entry were removed and replaced with

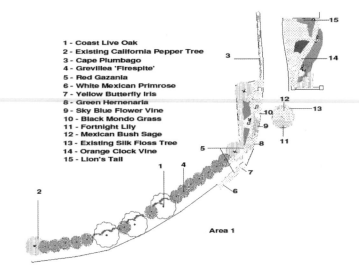

1 - Coast Live Oak
2 - Existing California Pepper Tree
3 - Cape Plumbago
4 - Grevillea 'Firespite'
5 - Red Gazania
6 - White Mexican Primrose
7 - Yellow Butterfly Iris
8 - Green Hernenaria
9 - Sky Blue Flower Vine
10 - Black Mondo Grass
11 - Fortnight Lily
12 - Mexican Bush Sage
13 - Existing Silk Floss Tree
14 - Orange Clock Vine
15 - Lion's Tail

Area 1

Ill. 8-11. Area 1 is the entry to the property.

colorful shrubs that block views to the corral. Shrubs and ground cover in reds, purples, grays, and white reduce the glare of the concrete drive and entry walls.

At the entry is a round raised planter representing the metal element. Here is where the "river" motif begins with red Gazania. The shape of the river motif represents the water element. The trees are all considered to be Wood elements. Of course the red color and some of the sword-shaped plants represent the Fire element. Punctuating the "river" are rocks to reinforce the Earth element and bring stability to the clients.

At the entry the Six True Colors were employed to start the energy in the right direction. This is a powerful color sequence that represents the mantra Om Ma Ni Pad Me Hum in the colors white, red, yellow, green, blue, and black. At the entry we start with White Mexican Primrose and then repeat Red Gazania, then move to a different texture with Yellow Butterfly

Iris and then decreasing in size to Green Hernaria, then to Blue Sky Flower Vine, and finally to Black Mondo Grass.

One of the most important solutions, deflecting the street's downhill pressure, was already partially in place. A round raised planter planted with an existing beautiful Silk Floss tree deflects the fast-moving energy of the street. On the tree, a convex mirror was added to embrace the entire street. The client was advised to shave the thorns from the trunk of the tree to avoid the poison arrows that the tree produces. To create a meaningful motif, the planter was designed in the yin-yang shape using white flowering Fortnight Lily, which accentuates Yang energy by pointing at the sky, and purple flowering Mexican Bush Sage, whose flowers flow like water.

After passing the entry gates, the "river" gradually shifts to orange. As with any transition you want to carry the plants from one area to overlap into the next. So the Red Gazania continues for a while in this space while we also start the transition to Orange Clock Vine as the groundcover and Lion's Tail as one of the shrubs.

Principles for the Entry Area

The feng shui principles used for this entry space are:

Colorful plantings especially red, to attract ch'i

Plants used to attract life force, such as, birds

Trees, shrubs, and vines along the borders used to "fill in" the missing areas with vitality.

Open up the front entry area.

Five elements balanced at front entry.

Street relationship smoothed by rounded planter corrected with a mirror.

Career Gua enhanced with amorphous patterns of plant masses and plants that attract birds to pique the sense of hearing, including Pines, Mexican Bush Sage, and Gazania.

Helpful People represented by the gray foliaged Mexican Bush Sage and interesting shaped rocks used to enhance this area.

Area 2 – Second Impression and a Secret Spot

Upon entering the property, the sight ahead is a bare slope uphill crowned with the house at the top. The client initially did not want to invest in developing this slope. A barren slope is a negative condition in both feng shui and landscape practices. A lack of plants indicates a paucity of ch'i in feng shui terms and the slope is subject to erosion in landscape terms. The river motif is continued through this area. An isolated pine wooded area adjacent to the missing Knowledge Gua seemed like a perfect spot for a private meditation space.

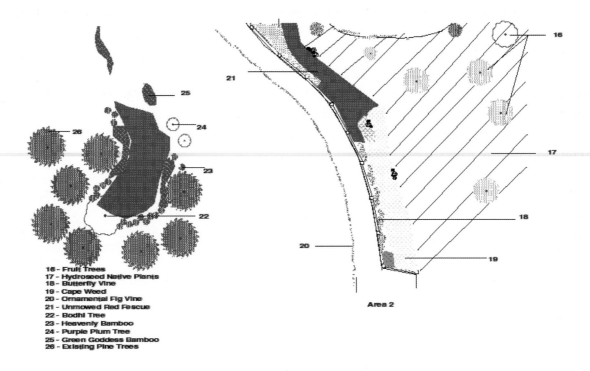

16 – Fruit Trees
17 – Hydroseed Native Plants
18 – Butterfly Vine
19 – Cape Weed
20 – Ornamental Fig Vine
21 – Unmowed Red Fescue
22 – Bodhi Tree
23 – Heavenly Bamboo
24 – Purple Plum Tree
25 – Green Goddess Bamboo
26 – Existing Pine Trees

Ill. 8-12. Area 2 is the slope up to toward the house.

The feng shui goals in this area were:

To continue the energy stream up toward the house.
To convert the barren slope in an economically feasible manner.
To add more baffling from the winds for the house.
To create a cohesive, interesting, and spiritual retreat for the private meditation area.

The solutions begin with the slope located in the Career Gua. To provide a low-cost method of covering the slope, it was decided to hydroseed the area with native perennials and shrubs that would provide colorful plants with soil holding ability. In addition to the random pattern of plants that expresses the water element, Gazanias, California Encelia, Coreopsis, and

140

Desert Marigold attract birds which enhance the sense of hearing. In staggered spacing, fruit trees are included on the slope to increase the productiveness of the space. These trees also baffle the fierce winds. Varieties of fruit trees included Tangerine, Orange, Tamarind, Apple, Macadamia, Plum Trees, Mango, and Pineapple Guava. Fruit trees connect the property to the roots of this land as an agricultural area and to the fertility of the surrounding agrarian valley. From the house, the addition of fruit trees allows the client to "borrow in agricultural land" from the valley below.

The energy stream continues first with continuity from the orange area and then with the yellow and green colored ground covers in the stream. Cape Weed was used as the yellow ground-cover for its drought resistance and beautiful yellow flowers. Because the wall is formidable directly facing the entry, vines were added to drape over the wall and soften the blocking effect and glare. The vine used to represent the yellow area is the aggressive, lush Butterfly Vine. As we move up to the green space, unmowed Red Fescue Grass is used as the groundcover and the hearty ornamental Fig Vine is used as the wall covering.

The area selected for a private meditation spot is a hidden bare spot surrounded by pine trees. The client wanted a lush and meaningful "room" to enjoy. The plants selected for this space all have deep connections to the Asian influences that nurture the client's spirit. The plants used here are Golden Goddess Bamboo, Heavenly Bamboo, Purple Leafed Plum, and a Bodhi Tree. The Bodhi Tree is most appropriately used here in the Knowledge Gua and as a mark of a serious commitment to enlightenment. The Pines that grow here are used to complete the missing part of the Knowledge Gua.

___

Principles for the Second Impression

The feng shui principles used in the design of this space were:

Connection to the history of the land and the surrounding environs.

Opening the constrictive feeling of the wall with vines.

Restoring ch'i to the slope by replanting it with native vegetation which will encourage wildlife and prevent erosion.

Plants that represent the Helpful People area in this area are the Gazania and Desert Marigold and Pineapple Guava.

Previously planted Pines are also associated with Helpful People.

The Career Gua is represented by the shapes of plant massing, the bird-attracting plants in the hydro-seed mix, Plum Trees, and Blackberry Vines.

The Knowledge Gua is represented by all of the plants in the meditation space used to foster enlightenment.

Area 3 - Upper Slope and House Environs

The grounds on the flat pad around the home are the most highly used and most closely related to the family's daily activities. Surrounding the home are a gazebo, pool, spa, tennis court, alligator pond, desert turtle area, and side yard. The beginning of the entry walkway from the motor court and the side yard will be discussed in Area 4. The previous property owners did much of the planting on the house pad. The major challenge was creating an inviting front entry. The existing plantings of juniper were overgrown and blocked the walkways. The existing palms create dark corners for the rooms that look out onto the entry court.

The upper slope is a visible precipice seen from the tennis court and pool and spa area. The client didn't want much planting on the slope but wanted to look down on attractive views.

The feng shui goals in this area were:

Design a space that enhances and draws energy to the front door.
Remove or trim all overgrown plants that block light to the house interior inside.
Add planting to fallow areas.
Add pots to the pool deck to enliven the space.
Make a "green screen" of the tennis court fence. Because of its proximity to the house, it blocks the energy at that side.
Increase the life force and the food production in the tortoise area so they can be fed from plants in or near the area.
Design an attractive environment for the alligator.
Enhance the upper slope and provide delightful views from the house pad.

At the house level, I designed the plantings around the house to support the areas of the Ba-Gua. Even though the house is almost entirely in the Career area of the property, we can support the different areas of the house Ba-Gua using the colors and elements. The house entry is in the Career area. One logical option was to design a water feature and fish-pond to enhance the Career area and add harmony to the house. Its sound and energy attracts people and ch'i to the front door. The water feature is charming, appearing to stream under the entry walk and embrace the entry with good luck. Plantings of Ferns, Carpet Bugle, Gardenia, Blue Lily Turf, and Horsetail further improve the space with fragrance, protection, and balance. Across the entry overhang, Blood Red Trumpet Vine attracts auspicious ch'i. To cap it off, a wind chime is added to complete the space and add one more harmonious element.

The existing plantings around the house are trimmed to allow more light in the house. Planters next to the house use plants that would remain manageable and offer fragrance and color. Plants in the Helpful People area include the gray foliage Lavender. Near the Children's area is the fragrant Giant Burmese Honeysuckle. Its fragrance ties into the metal element in the Children's area and brings the earth element color in to support this area. Though roof covered, the house is missing the Children's area. To correct this problem, a bird bath with a fanciful

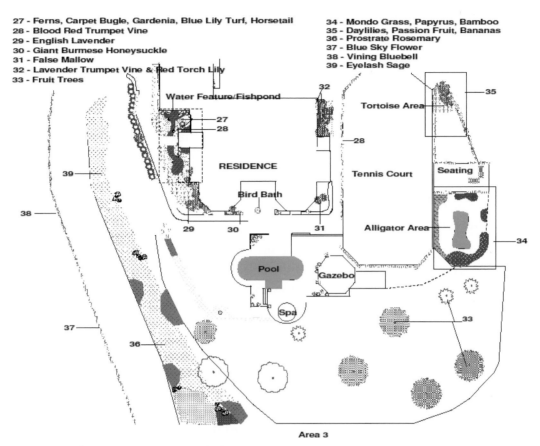

27 - Ferns, Carpet Bugle, Gardenia, Blue Lily Turf, Horsetail
28 - Blood Red Trumpet Vine
29 - English Lavender
30 - Giant Burmese Honeysuckle
31 - False Mallow
32 - Lavender Trumpet Vine & Red Torch Lily
33 - Fruit Trees

34 - Mondo Grass, Papyrus, Bamboo
35 - Daylilies, Passion Fruit, Bananas
36 - Prostrate Rosemary
37 - Blue Sky Flower
38 - Vining Bluebell
39 - Eyelash Sage

Ill. 8-13. Area 3 is the area closest to the house.

metal sculpture was placed in alignment with the walls. The rooms around the "empty" space look out to this delightful solid cure and the pool area beyond. To enliven the area near the pool, pots of red and yellow flowering succulents, sunrose, and annual plants are used. To enhance the Relationship area is the pink flowering False Mallow. The tennis court is close to the house and needs to be screened so we used the Blood Red Trumpet Vine here as the Fame area of the house looks out onto it. The vitality of this voluptuous vine will add "space" between the house and tennis court. Around the Wealth area are purple flowering Lavender Trumpet Vine and red Torch Ginger. The last two areas around the house are addressed in Area 4 discussion.

The upper slope like the lower slope is planted with fruit trees. Trees like Fig, Papaya, Cherry, Star Fruit, and Guava will not only offer the fruit but also frame the valley views from the pool deck.

The tortoise and alligator areas are on the other side of the tennis court and are separated by a latticed seating area. Both areas require open space to allow for the free movement of the animals. The alligator area already has a pond, and a waterfall is added to keep the water fresh. Plantings used are for texture and interest and to offer a backdrop for the novelty of watching the alligator. In the foreground, Mondo Grass was used, with Papyrus and Bamboo used as backdrops. In the tortoise area, Daylilies, Passion Fruit, and Banana trees, all edible, attractive plants, double to feed people and pets. Grapes are planted over the arbor as another food source and Pink Flowering Jasmine along the tennis court fence offers abundant fragrance.

The rainbow-colored stream continues along the driveway through this area with Prostrate Rosemary as a groundcover and Blue Sky Flower Vine along the wall. As the "river" moves up to the color indigo, we move to the lovely Vining Bluebell as the cover for the wall and a mass of eye-popping Eyelash Sage.

Principles for the Upper Slope and House Environs

The feng shui principles used in the design of this space were:

A water feature and wind chime to enhance the Career area of the house.
Fruiting Trees planted on the slope to lift the ch'i in the slope area.
Add ch'i to the house by trimming overgrown foliage.
Enliven the pool deck with colorful plantings.
Balance out the reptile areas with plantings that provide taste, texture, and fragrance.
Plants used to enhance the Knowledge area include the Sky Flower Vine, Australian Bluebells, Prostrate Rosemary, Eyelash Sage, and an existing Olive Tree.
The Career sector contains the pool, spa, and part of the new water feature. The fruit trees on the slope, Lavender and Giant Honeysuckle will attract birds.
The Helpful People area is enhanced with Pines, rocks, and the tortoise and alligators that are good objects of contemplation.
Complete the missing Children's area of the house with sturdy bird bath.

Area 4 - Office and Motor court Area

The office and motor court areas are of utmost importance to this family unit. Attracting positive ch'i to the office will add business to sustain the family and create a supportive work atmosphere. Included in this area are a substantial slope and retaining wall viewed from the client's workroom. In general, hills behind a house support the home and are very good feng shui; however, this one feels overbearing. Also included in this area is the very important entry walk leading to the front door and a secondary entry to the house used informally which originate from the motor court.

The feng shui goals in this area are:

To draw ch'i to the office and the entry walk for the house.
To provide a lively and beautiful view from the office workspace.
To provide visual relief from the heat and glare of the motor court.
To offer a beautiful view of the house side yard garden and secondary entrance.

To meet the Feng shui goals we begin with the walkways to the home and office. At the house walk entry, a center planter is filled with purple statice, white star jasmine, yellow sunrose, and rocks to connect this area to the "river" and stabilize the area. As a backdrop silhouetted against the house is a spectacular fragrant yellow angel's trumpet vine.

The entrance to the office is enlivened with red bougainvillea and red sage. The bougainvillea is set against the walls of the office so they aren't hazardous to visitors and the red sage is in the planter directly in front of the front door so that there is no strong element opposing the door.

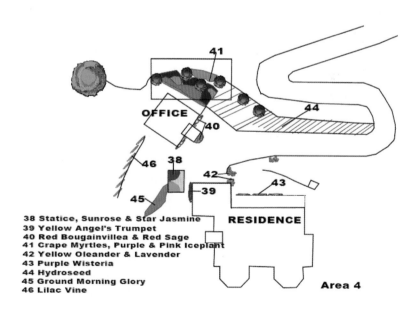

38 Statice, Sunrose & Star Jasmine
39 Yellow Angel's Trumpet
40 Red Bougainvillea & Red Sage
41 Crape Myrtles, Purple & Pink Iceplant
42 Yellow Oleander & Lavender
43 Purple Wisteria
44 Hydroseed
45 Ground Morning Glory
46 Lilac Vine

Ill. 8-14. Area 4 is the area close to the house and around the office.

Yellow sunrose on the ground plane visually connects the office entry to the house entry. The existing fountain in front of the office completes and enhances the Career area for the office. Of course, the water pours toward the entry. Here again a wind chime is added to the front of the office door to attract ch'i.

On the slope visible from the workroom, bold patterns of hot pink and purple ice plant add artistic relief. Crape myrtles in the same shades on the slope reduced the perceived height of the slope. These beautiful summer flowering trees also offer welcome shade. Ivy Geraniums cascade over the wall, reducing the blocking effect of it, and pots of varying heights on the patio both help hide the wall and add focal points of interest.

A secondary entrance to the house is accessed either through the motor court or the rear of the garage. Bright yellow oleanders flank the entry from the motor court to a grassy side yard surrounded with color. The gray Provence lavender supports the Helpful People area of the house. The slope behind is hydroseeded with the same mixture as at the entry to the property.

The "river" ends near the entry with the purple Ground Morning Glory and Lilac Vine along the retaining wall

Behind the office is a knoll that overlooks the valley and includes views to the ocean. Another small meditation space is located here with an overhead structure planted with Wisteria for winter color and fragrance. This space offers the family a place to get away from the activity of the office and an opportunity to expand one's horizons. When you gaze out over an ocean your energy is not confined by any limits. It floats everywhere the currents take it. An Elm tree, which is believed to foster contact with nature spirits, anchors the space.

Principles for the Office and Motor Court Areas

The feng shui principles used in the design of this space were:

The use of red auspicious plants and wind chime to attract ch'i to the office entry.

Brightly colored plants draw energy together and rocks stabilize energy at the house entry. Fragrance entices people and good energy in.

The workspace views patterns of pink and purple, the colors for Wealth and Relationship. The plantings added to all of the spaces that surround the motor court are designed to balance the heat and glare. Rocks are used to stabilize the yang energy and purple and blue also balance the yang energy.

The Knowledge Gua of the property in this area is enhanced with the use of the Ground Morning Glory. The meditation space in this area can be used to expand the owner's spiritual horizons.

The Career Gua of the space is enhanced by the water-like patterns emphasized in this area. Another slope in this area will be hydroseeded and will attract birds and bees. Wisteria, Wild Lilac, Santa Barbara Daisy, Foxglove, and existing Lantana all attract birds.

Example Four: A Design of the Heart

This series of projects was produced with the counsel of His Holiness Grandmaster Lin Yun for Lin Yun Temple and the Lin Yun Cultural Center in Berkeley, California. The designs use very few common landscape tools such as plants, relying on sacred symbols and their prime placement for optimal energy enhancement. Though you may be unfamiliar with the symbols, I wanted to include an example that would give you a novel approach to your land. Your land can actually be viewed like a canvas to be filled with life-affirming images that support whatever aspect you may need.

The Sites

There are two sites that are part of the Yun Lin Temple. The Temple is a majestic building with many steps leading up to the front door and the back is a flat, largely asphalt area. There are plantings on the perimeter and sides of the building. The Yun Lin Cultural Center is slightly elevated from the street with planting in the front, largely asphalt in the back, and planting in some side areas of the back. The ideas for the project were hatched and implemented over a series of years.

One day I was standing in the back of the Yun Lin Cultural Center and thinking how regrettable it was there was only asphalt there when I suddenly saw the image of a Dharma Wheel impressed on the asphalt. I saw people walking on the wheel and experiencing an uplifted spirit.

The Dharma Wheel is composed of what is known as the six true words, Om Ma Ni Pad Me Hum, each of which has a respective color: white, red, yellow, green, blue, black. The mantra can be interpreted in many ways and on many levels, even from culture to culture. Its base is Buddhist and though there is no literal translation, it is thought to be the acknowledgment that enlightenment is already within us all. The word "Dharma" represents Buddha's teachings and the wheel represents the various types of teaching that

Buddha gave. The Dharma Wheel, in the context of Black Sect Tantric Buddhism, can be used as a blessing, a protection, and a method for removing negativity from an environment. Setting it in motion or spinning the Dharma Wheel amps up the energy one hundred fold. Each syllable becomes the center for another set of the mantra so the energy spins inward and outward to infinity.

When I proposed the idea to His Holiness Grandmaster Lin, he tweaked and corrected my original format and approved all of the exact colors that were to be used in the implementa-

tion. The Constantly Turning Dharma Wheel spins around the Tai Chi, the symbol of perfect balance. The image is further balanced as the large mantra spins counterclockwise and the mantras around each syllable spin clockwise. Though I had never done anything like this before, the image of the completed venture carried me through. I and five others did the work during a silent retreat period of five days. Here you see the result.

Buoyed by a successful project, the next year we picked another space and image. I thought we could use the image of the Ten Coins of the Ching Dynasty to lead people to the front door of Yun Lin Temple. The coins represent all the wealth of the wealthiest Chinese Dynasty. They are used to attract auspiciousness and wealth, to ward off evil spirits, and to help one's career and life path. My original design was simple – three sets of coins starting at the bottom of the stairs and leading up to the top of the stairs. Those plans were quickly revised

by His Holiness, who advised nine sets of coins leading up to the front door of the temple and Six True Word mantra wheels at the landings on the way up. The coins are designed to overlap each other so the force of energy is not broken between them, and "red string" makes the connection.

In the back of the temple I proposed to add the image of the Five Buddha Firecrackers, which lend support, power, and protection to the Fame, Wealth and Relationship areas of the property. They can be used anywhere you want to explode forward or remove obstacles in your life. The ritual ones produced by Yun Lin Temple have His Holiness's calligraphy for the word "Buddha" on them to add to their power. In this design, again I thought too small. The usual format for the Five Buddha Firecrackers is five firecrackers put together in an arrowhead shape. We ended up doubling the size of the firecrackers and increasing the number to nine. They are an impressive sight and serve as a protective vision at the back of the temple.

The next project we took on was adding the Ten Ching Dynasty coins to the front of the Yun Lin Cultural Center. This time because we had a smaller space and wanted to cover up an unattractive paint job, we added the background of gold, the Chinese emperor's color, behind the coins. This adds another powerful dimension to the cure. We only used three sets of coins in this motif and added the red string between each of the coins. The walkway was too small for the Dharma wheel so we used the Tai Chi symbol in the middle.

In addition to the coins we used the powerful motif of two dragons playing with a pearl. The hedges were carved into dragons on both sides of the walkway. It is difficult to see the heads in this picture as years have left them with less definition. The next picture shows an earlier time when you can see the dragon's head as well as the undulations of the dragon's back. Above the door we placed a convex mirror to represent the pearl. It also has the effect of doubling the coins and expanding the scope of vision for the temple.

We also did some planting at the Cultural Center. The Wealth corner needed to be cleaned up and an apartment building loomed over that corner as well as along the Children and Relationship areas. We decided to plant Timber Bamboo to provide a buffer from the neighboring buildings. The plants also offer strength and flexibility to those aspects of the temple. Two fruit trees were already in the Wealth corner and we added more. While people were working in the Wealth corner they came up with a brilliant addition to the plan. They added a seating area and a symbol of Yungdrung on the ground. This symbol which means "eternal," has its roots in the Bon Tradition, a sect older than Buddhism from Tibet. The roots of Yun Lin Temple are in the Bon tradition so it was a natural to add that to the composition.

On the wall you can see calligraphy. His Holiness Grandmaster Lin Yun was a master calligrapher. He added poems that he composed himself to add to the wall here. I was so touched that he used his time and talent to honor our efforts.

One of the poems in this calligraphy seen above on the right translates:

Flowers now blooming in the barren back yard
Gratitude to my fellow practitioners for their care and effort
Meditate here, dawn and dusk
And luck blossoms upon gradual and instant realization.

This last example introduced several new spiritual concepts. The last chapter is all about spiritual practices, ceremonies done on the land to protect, consecrate, and uplift the land and the owners. These are very powerful ceremonies and they bring to life the Three Secret Reinforcement that we learned about in the beginning of the book.

Chapter 9

Special Cures and Ceremonies on the Land

Ceremonies have always been done to mark important aspects of a human life, including birth, death, and everything in between. With the uncertainties of harvests, ceremonies are a way to court favor from the Earth Gods. When a new house was built feng shui masters and astrologers were consulted for the most auspicious time and place for the building, and ceremonies were conducted to seek the blessings of the Earth Gods.

What do we do if we buy a piece of land or a house that has had an unfortunate past? Are we doomed to suffer the same fate as the previous owners, be it bankruptcy, divorce, or death? There are special blessing ceremonies meant to purge the land of past bad energy and sow the seeds of good luck.

We have already learned that the Three Secret Reinforcement is a crucial part of successful feng shui work. This ceremony should be a component of each ceremony and the special cures that we will review in this chapter.

Special cures in this chapter are used to counteract feng shui that comes from the unbalanced placement of elements and are designed to allow us to flourish with elements that would normally cause us problems because of their negative feng shui implications.

A Basic Formula

In Chapter 4, I introduced the Three Secret Reinforcement which is an essential part of any ceremony that you conduct. This is a review and deeper look at this important component:

1. **BODY SECRET**: Use ritual hand gestures ("mudras") to involve the body in the ceremony.

I have discussed the Heart Calming Mudra and would also like to introduce the Expelling Mudra. The Expelling Mudra both removes bad luck and invites in auspiciousness. To do it you grab your middle and ring fingers with your thumb, leaving your index and baby fingers extended. Then you flick by extending the restrained fingers. Do this nine times for the Body Secret part.

2. **SPEECH SECRET**: A prayer or mantra recited nine times. Many of my Catholic friends and clients use Hail Mary here while my Jewish friends and clients may use the Shama. Again, anything that is most comfortable and meaningful to you is what is most appropriate. My favorite is the Six Syllable Mantra, Om Ma Ni Pad Me Hum because it carries the vision of enlightenment, however when I am doing a ceremony to protect a property that has been haunted I use a mantra that places guardians around the land for protection.

3. **MIND SECRET**: Visualization and mystic intent. Here you want to fully see what you want to correct or change with the ceremony. If you are doing the ceremony to deflect the negative energy of a building pointing at your front door, imagine protection plus the other hopes and dreams you want to enter through that door. For instance, if you want your company to improve, visualize the company at its present state and then see it doing better and better until it is exactly what you want. The process of going from present state to the desired state is important in your visualization. Make your visualizations as detailed as possible.

One of the most widely used formulas for ceremonies is cinnabar rice. Cinnabar is a powder primarily used for medicinal use in China; however, in the context of our ceremonies, it is used to expel evil ch'i and invite in auspiciousness. In ancient China cinnabar was thought to be the elixir of immortality and was used by emperors seeking to live forever. Obtaining cinnabar isn't always an easy venture. In the United States, it may be hard to get. Its Chinese name is Ju Sha or Zhu Sha and it is sometimes carried in Chinese pharmacies. You may also find some Internet sources for it.

Rice in the mixture is symbolic of abundance. In most of the world, if you have rice to put in your pot, you are indeed fortunate. The strong liquor is used to ward off evil spirits.

To make cinnabar rice for blessings, fill a bowl three-quarters full of rice. If you have a large project (home or property) to bless, use a large bowl. For huge properties, you may need more than one bowl. To the bowl of uncooked rice, add cinnabar powder. How much you add is a matter of how much rice you have. If you have a lot of rice, you may need to use a teaspoon of cinnabar or more. It will turn the rice red when the process is complete. Open a new bottle of high-proof liquor and add nine capfuls of liquor to the mixture. An alternative method is to

His Holiness Grandmaster Lin Yun and Her Holiness Khadro Crystal Chu preparing cinnabar rice using the Three Secret Reinforcement ceremony

add the number of drops equal to your Chinese age (your age plus one). If the ceremony is for a husband and wife you could add the ages together, use the husband's age, or use 99 drops of liquor in the mixture. To mix, use the middle finger of the right hand if you are male or left hand if you are female. When you use the middle finger, the other fingers are held horizontally. This is a special mudra called the Vajra mudra. It adds extra power to the process. While you are mixing you want to visualize the light of the universe or 10,000 Buddhas diving into the mix and you should recite the Six Syllable Mantra (Om Ma Ni Pad Me Hum) 108 times. This makes for an incredibly powerful mixture.

Tree Cures

Here I would like to review the various tree cures that I have offered in previous chapters and give you some new cures that will be useful as you work in the garden.

When a tree is located directly in front of a door, it blocks the energy and prevents it from coming in. You have to judge whether the tree is close enough to actually block the entry. Sometimes that is an easy determination but other times it isn't. If the tree is far away, for instance, across the street, it won't have a blocking effect. If you have a blocking tree, get a brand new black pen. Cut a circle from a piece of new red paper and while holding your breath write the words *Raise head, see happiness* with the black pen and affix this to the tree at eye level.

153

Sometimes we have to remove a tree from our property. I have had clients who wanted to add more space to their houses or had to remove a tree that was invading their sewers. Whatever the reason, removing a tree is a big undertaking in terms of the energy on your property. All trees serve to enhance the energy on a property, in fact, transforming from low energy to auspicious energy. Trees are entities to be revered and thanked for their restoration of good energy. Before demolishing a tree, mix cinnabar rice with 99 drops of liquor as described above, and spread it around the base of the tree. When you are doing this ceremony, imagine the spirit of the tree moving on to a new and better life experience. Thank the spirit of the tree for being there and helping your home, property, and family.

What happens when a tree on your property, especially one near your front door, dies? Dead trees must be cured quickly. The potential effect of a dead tree at the front door is that a person may die or, suffer illness, bankruptcy, or business decline. I have a personal story to share about this. In this picture you see the pitiful dead tree confronting the front door of my in-laws' house. The tree was much loved by my father-in-law, who planted it personally and propped it up every time the wind blew it over. Its decline mirrored his. This picture was taken right after he died and my mother-in-law became ill. This is not the only case I have seen. Many times when a person calls me out to work on the feng shui of a house, I can see the story in the landscape of the previous owner's decline or demise. There are a few methods you can use to cure the dead tree on a property. One is to sprinkle a mixture of cinnabar rice around the trunk of the tree and then lead the cinnabar rice in a path to the front door. This honors the position of the tree and its relationship to the house. The other way to cure this situation is to "restore" its vitality by twining a vine or even an artificial plant around the tree. It is better to add a fruiting or flowering plant, either artificial or real. This method reestablishes life force to the tree. A third method of curing a dead tree is to saw off the dead trunk of the tree and place a potted live plant on the stump.

Tree trimming can be a serious difficulty for you as well. It can affect your limbs because if you chop too much the plant will get its revenge. I always communicate with any plants I am trimming to let them know what I am doing and why I am doing it. The day before I begin trimming I sit with the plant to explain what I am doing and ask for its help in the process. Then while I do the trimming I maintain a meditative state so that I am in constant contact with the spirit of the tree. When I get to the aesthetic shaping, I ask the tree to direct me to its imbalances so that I can correct them and make it even more beautiful. For a novice, if you have never done this communication, it may seem strange or intimidating. The more you work with plants, caring for them, the more you will tune into their energy. When I come home from a trip nowadays, as soon as I step onto my property, I ask if any plant needs anything. I usually get a sense of which plants need water or food right away. It is a matter of caring and wanting to communicate. As for a transcendental cure, if you have trimmed a tree, use a cinnabar rice mixture to surround the tree and make a line to the door of your house so it will feel like it is part of the family.

Other Elements on the Property

One important element that I haven't discussed in reviewing the feng shui of the lot is the other buildings on the lot and their effect on the luck of the owners. If you have a closed structure such as a tool shed or garage in the Wealth, Fame, or Relationship areas it can limit your potential in those areas of your life. An open structure like a gazebo has no effect on your luck. In other Ba-gua areas of the lot, a tool shed can be beneficial; for instance, located in the Knowledge area, a tool shed will make knowledge your tool.

If you have a tool shed in the Wealth corner, you can place a fan on the roof to lift the energy. If you have a garage in the Wealth corner, it may actually be beneficial for you as you can bring Wealth home every time you drive into the garage, but it still needs to be "cured." If the building is in the Relationship corner one member of the partnership may establish a "home" elsewhere. If a building, either closed or open, is near the house in the Children's area, it limits the potential for your child's advancement.

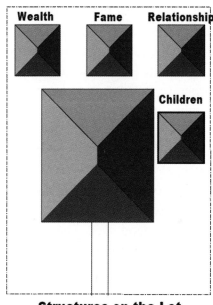

Structures on the Lot

To cure outbuildings in unlucky areas, you can do a ceremony where you toss cinnabar rice around the outbuilding and bring it to the door of the house as if you are lassoing the building and connecting it to the house. If you can't get all the way around the out-building because it is too close to the property line you can make a trail of the cinnabar rice from the door of the outbuilding to the closest door of the house. In effect you are making the out-building part of the house. Another way to connect the building to the house is to paint a red line with paint that has cinnabar powder in it to the house. A third method of connecting the two buildings is to have a light on the outbuilding that shines back to the roof of the house. Of these methods, the second is the most effective.

Planting a Foundation, New Construction, and Clearing Property Cures

Most of the ceremonies we do are transcendental solutions. Mundane problems that we experience can be cured by transcendental solutions, making these ceremonies we do very important. In other words, by showing respect and service to the land we can reverse the effect of our mundane human problems.

There are certain situations where ceremonies are always recommended. When you begin construction, lay the foundation for a building, complete construction, move into a new property, or have a run of bad luck, a ceremony is important to either positively start a venture or to shift negative ch'i to positive. Why do we need ceremonies in these situations? When we do construction or erect buildings we are ripping open the earth. Tearing open the land or our house exposes us to the possibility of attracting bad spirits to the chaos that is always there during construction. Any time we enter into construction, we need to communicate with the land and the Earth Gods to make peace.

This Site Purification ceremony is done when you are building a new structure, remodeling a structure, or moving to a new house. When you perform this ceremony, construction goes smoothly and it insures peace and luck after you move in.

1. Preparation:

a. Gather a measure of cinnabar, a new bottle of high-proof liquor, and uncooked rice. How much cinnabar is used will depend on the amount of rice that is needed. Add the cinnabar to a bowl of uncooked rice and add nine drops, nine capfuls, or nine cups of distilled spirits from a new bottle of liquor. Look at the rice as if it were a person and thank it for helping you do this good deed. The rice and other ingredients are your helpers. Talk to the liquor and cinnabar powder and thank them for helping you cleanse the site.

b. Prepare fresh oranges. Peel or cut nine round pieces (about the size and shape of a quarter) of orange peels from each of nine oranges. Tear the orange peels into small pieces. Talk to the oranges to thank them for helping you cleanse the site and bring auspiciousness to it. If the site is large, you can use eighteen or twenty-seven oranges instead of nine.

2. Mix the above two items together. Stir it with your middle finger until they form an even mixture. This is the same Vajra mudra that we discussed in the preparation of cinnabar rice. As you stir, perform Three Secret Reinforcement. For the speech part of the Three Secret Reinforcement you can either chant ten different mantras or the Six Syllable Mantra (Om Ma Ni Pad Me Hum) 108 times.

3. Recite Body, Speech, and Mind Purification Mantras each three times. These mantras are used to help us purify the karma that we have incurred from our body, speech, and mind over all the lifetimes we have lived. These mantras are a very powerful way to clear all aspects of negative karma, not only personally but also for the house and land that we inhabit.

Body Purification Mantra:

An xiuduoli xiuduoli, xiumoli xiumoli suopohe (pronounced Un show dowlee, show dowlee, sho mowlee, show mowlee, sew po ha)

Speech Purification Mantra:

An xiuli xiuli, moh xiuli, xiuxiuli, suopohe (pronounced Un showlee, showlee, moha showlee, show showlee, sew po ha)

Mind Purification Mantra:

An warila daheheho (pronounced Un wah lee law da huh huh ho)

4. Visualize myriad Buddhas or white light coming down to this site and your favorite deity or god coming onto the land. Project your own ch'i in front of that deity or Buddha and pay your respects to the Buddha or deity. Visualize merging your ch'i with the Buddha or deity's ch'i. You have the Buddha's wisdom, Buddha's compassion, and Buddha's power. Bring your ch'i and Buddha's ch'i back into your body so that it is the Buddha or deity within you performing the ceremony.

5. Sprinkle the orange and cinnabar rice mixture using the Giving Mudra (palm facing up) outwards toward all eight directions. The Giving Mudra is a motion with your palm up and projecting out from your body on a level or slightly upward motion. Visualize that this will feed the roaming spirits so that they will not disturb the site, and expel all inauspicious ch'i. You will ward off the yin ch'i and bad luck ch'i. All the negative ch'i will be gone.

6. Sprinkle the orange and cinnabar rice mixture using the Seeding Mudra (palm facing down) toward all eight directions. This Seeding toss sows the seeds of blessedness so that you are sowing the seeds of auspiciousness, prosperity, good health, and happiness. Visualize Buddha's or deities light fills the entire site.

7. Throw three handfuls of the mixture up into the air over your head, visualize myriad rays of Buddha's or deities light filling the site and people.

First Throw: Visualize it carries auspicious light to cover the people and structure like an umbrella. This auspicious rice, together with deities' or Buddha's light, covers the structure, all the family members, and all the people that work in the place. This purifies and elevates the energy of the people and brings good luck, good health, and prosperity.

Second Throw: Visualize elevating the energy in your community and its residents and bless the entire nation and its people.

Third Throw: Blessing for world peace, the well-being of all human beings, and all sentient beings to liberate them from suffering.

A Powerful Esoteric Cure

I once had difficulty with my shoulder and visited a chiropractor who adjusted me. The adjustment seemed to work and I was pain free for a day or two, but within a few days the pain returned. At my next appointment, he reevaluated the situation, insisting that adjustments always work so perhaps there was some other basis for my problem. He advised me to reorder the way I was sleeping and the pain disappeared. I tell this story because sometimes I have done a clearing for a property and I can see the energy is better and flowing but for some reason the change doesn't seem to manifest. Sometimes this will happen because other plans need time to manifest, but other times it is because the energy of the land needs to be shifted in another way. Sometimes the gate to the land is stuck like a broken record and can't play the song until the needle is moved. This cure is about moving the needle.

Visualize a spinning disc like a lazy susan in a Chinese restaurant divided into eight sections that are turning constantly clockwise. When you step onto the property, determine which door you have stepped into with your intuition. The eight parts of the eight-door wheel are Life, Cease, Hope, Instability, Death, Scenery, Improvement, and Injury. The meaning of those words for the purpose of this cure is: Life - the best, Hope - very good, Injury - not good, weakening of life and hope, Improvement - slowly making recovery, Scenery - good prospect is on the way, Death - worst, stopping of hope, Instability - not as bad as death but frightening, Cease - turning from good to bad.

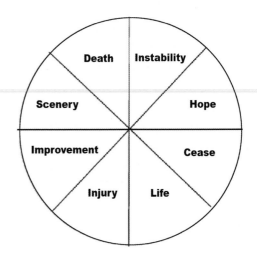

Eight door wheel

Once you have determined which part of the wheel is at the front, you know where the area of Life is. Walk over to the door of life and perform the Three Secret Reinforcement, gather the energy in the life area, and then visualize that you are carrying life to each of the eight positions one by one in a clockwise manner. Next, to cement the change, plant trees in the areas that previously were bad: death, injury, cease, and instability. Evergreen trees with fruits and/or flowers are preferred.

I must confess that when I started to practice this cure, I didn't have the confidence to see what was in front of me. When I felt this cure was the one that should be performed, instead of trusting my intuition when I was to step onto the property, I used dowsing rods to confirm my initial reaction. Sometimes I even dowsed the property before I visited so I would have a plan of action. Before you get a feeling for the land, you may want to dowse to help you with this cure.

A Deeper Use of Color

In previous sections I discussed the Six Syllable Mantra (Om Ma Ni Pad Me Hum) and its power. It is multi layered and has deep significance. Each syllable has a color associated with it—white, red, yellow, green, blue, black, respectively. Note that in different cultures, the colors may be different for some of the syllables. It represents the six realms of cyclical existence that are the types of lives that beings cycle through - Heaven, Jealous Gods, Humans, Animals, Hungry Ghosts, Hell. It represents the six paramitas which are the perfections that can purify your past and present karma. They are Generosity, Discipline, Tolerance, Perseverance, Meditation, and Wisdom. Again, in different cultures you may see Generosity, Ethics, Patience, Diligence, Renunciation, and Wisdom, or variants. Buddha declared this is the most beneficial mantra of all. His Holiness the Dalai Lama translates the meaning of the mantra as "In dependence on the practice of a path which is an indivisible union of method and wisdom, you can transform your impure body, speech, and mind into the pure exalted body, speech, and mind of a Buddha."

With such history and deep meaning you can only imagine the influence a set of flags with these colors and meanings may have. Here is how to prepare them.

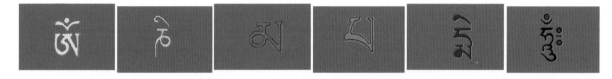

The individual colors of the six flags each correspond to the six colors of the Six Syllable Mantra. The seed mantra is written on each flag, either in Chinese, English, or Tibetan. One can also choose not to write the mantra on the flag and just use the color of the mantra of the flag. The flagpole should be made of bamboo.

To empower the flags, put them on your altar for at least nine days before installing them. Hold a mudra and then hold one flag, take a deep breath, and sharply exhale with the syllable of the mantra flag onto the flag. Visualize that the power of the mantra is attached to the flag and the auspicious color fills heaven and earth. Do the same for each of the six flags.

The size of the Six True Word Mantra flags may vary. You can hang smaller flags in your home or office. Bigger flags can be incorporated into the landscape design of public places such as gardens, airports, or harbors.

Flags can be used for 1. Feng shui adjustment, for instance if you want to emphasize your career or get a promotion. 2. Uplifting ch'i and the accumulation of luck; for instance, if you want to attract a mate. 3. The prevention of disaster; for instance, if you live in tornado country and want special protection. 4. If you have crows or other ill omens on your property, put the six mantra flags on the four perimeters of the property. 5. If your house is located near high-voltage power lines, transformer boxes, transmission towers, or garbage dumps, or if you want to protect yourself from a telephone pole. 6. If you have cemeteries, churches, police stations, hospitals, or other unlucky elements in the neighborhood, place the flags between you and the offending element. 7. They can also be used when you are doing construction of the building or in the yard in the back third of the house or lot. 8. They can be used to protect you in a cul-de-sac cure when used in your front yard.

Building Shrines Outside

A shrine is a holy place that is dedicated to the worship of a deity, saint, religion, ancestor, or idea. This could be an alcove to place your favorite religious deity or you could add a spot in your gazebo where you meditate. In Chinese culture most of the shrines are either for Mountain Gods or Earth Gods. Welcoming either of them onto your property will add a form of protection and luck for you.

Mountain shrines are usually larger and more public affairs than Earth shrines. Mountain shrines often honor the "Eastern Peak," one of the highest and holiest mountains in northern China. It was a place where the most influential writers and governments were located. There are shrines paying tribute to the Mountain Gods all over northern China. I have also seen the Taishan Mountain God represented as a beautiful rock that is standing tall, looking like a mountain.

Earth shrines are usually smaller and more personal. Throughout China there are different Earth Gods that people worship to protect their particular land. These protectors keep you safe from disasters, protect your accumulated wealth, and protect you from unsavory people.

I don't have an Earth god shrine on my property but I do have reminders of the things that I cherish around my property in the form of Buddha statues, St. Francis (protector of animals and plants), and beautiful art images that are important to me. I also have a few rocks that I think of as Taishan Mountain, one protecting my office and the other protecting my home entry. Find a way to honor the spiritual ideals that you value and make a place for them in your garden.

Conclusion

It is said that no two snowflakes are alike. Everything created by nature is unique, perfect, and impermanent. In creating our designs, when our images and intentions are clear, when we connect with our land, our design is bound to be perfect to manifest our objectives. There are no formulas or magic answers when you are working with nature. It is always challenging to begin a design. The best advice is to dive in and get started!

I have been talking all the way through the book about the need to start with an image. When I first began designing and didn't have much background, sometimes that meant looking at books and magazines to birth an inspiration. Sometimes the inspiration comes from sitting in a house and viewing the outdoors. When it is your personal yard there is often the tendency to overemphasize the importance of every single decision. Often moving into action is the thing that will help you build new and more creative ideas. The garden is a place where you can be bold. If you make a mistake with the planting part of it, you can make corrections. The garden is changeable and you should always view it as a canvas that can be painted over and redone.

The meaning and ideas for the garden don't have to be consistent throughout. You have seen gardens that I have designed that have some elements that move throughout the land and yet there is great variety from one area to another. Likewise, I have clients who have mixed spiritual ideas throughout their garden, Buddhist in one area and Merlin in another and yet Goddess in a third. The important thing about each garden is that it is a unique statement of what brings joy and beauty to that person.

When to Seek Help

There may come a time when you feel the need to collaborate on your ideas. Despite all of the guiding I have done in this book, you want an expert guide you in either the feng shui or the artistic direction for the plan. Perhaps you want to take the knowledge in this book and use it as a baseline for the helper that does the work for you.

Of course, the first thing I suggest is to find someone with whom you are comfortable. Sounds elementary but many people think that an expert has to be overbearing and dictatorial. My opinion is that the person is one to run from. Find someone who will listen and respect your ideas. If you have taken the time to read this book you have learned more than many professionals in either field.

In looking for a landscape expert, know that there are many different levels of designers. There are licensed landscape architects who are tested and qualified to work in all aspects of landscape design. There are landscape designers who can work on planting design and there are landscape contractors who are able to install landscape designs. There is some crossover. For instance, there are landscape designers who are very good at designing hardscape although in some states they are not legally allowed to do so, and there are many contractors who have great landscape design ideas. There are even firms that do both design and build and have people to work on all aspects with you. The important things that you need to evaluate are whether the person is a good listener so that they hear what you want and are willing to do what you want and that they have the design ability to enhance your initial ideas about your property.

When you are looking for a feng shui expert, remember what I mentioned about the different schools of feng shui. People from different schools will have different ideas about how to approach the landscape and what remedies may be used in different areas. They may use a compass or have other ideas about the geomancy of the land and how to balance it. Again, I advise that you find someone that you are comfortable with. This is your land and the worst feng shui solution is one that you hate looking at every day. If you are having an expert evaluate the inside of your home and you want them to work with you outside, unless you are just checking out a few ideas with them, I advise that you schedule a separate appointment for the landscape. I find it difficult to have the creative juice to do both interior and landscape in the same appointment unless the house and land are small or the suggestions needed are limited.

Creating Your Own Plan

One of the important concepts in landscape design is that of change. We are changing all the time. The you that is here right now isn't the you of even an hour ago. Plants are amazingly like us in that way. They are growing and constantly changing. I have had clients call me with alarm when their deciduous plants drop their leaves. I have reacted with surprise and alarm to see my plants drop leaves only to be overjoyed when they leaf out again. Life is change. Occasionally we expect a plant will grow to be eight feet tall to cover a fence only to realize after many years that it will never make it. Is it a dwarf or is the microclimate in the spot keeping it at a size that disappoints our dreams? Sometimes we plant a plant that we expect to be three feet high and when it is towering over us we realize that we have selected the monster of its race!

Though I think I am always aware of my spaces I may come home one day and see a hole in the landscape design or something that has overgrown a space or weeds that have taken hold that will require changes to a whole area of the garden. It is times like these that I am aware that I have made changes to my life and my point of view or my goals may have shifted. I may want to add, change, or amend my landscape to support the change coming to me.

Feng shui is the perfect tool to help with changes, whether they are big or small. Remember, you can never go wrong if you listen to the land and act from your heart. For those readers who have made it to this section of the book and still have doubts about whether feng shui will work, one of the greatest scientific minds of the world has reassurance. Albert Einstein said, "The most beautiful thing we can experience is the mysterious. It is the source of all true art and science."

About the Author

Shelley Sparks is a Feng Shui expert, licensed Landscape Architect and passionate gardener. Through the practices of Feng Shui and Landscape Design she creates harmony, healing and beneficial qualities to her client's home, business, and garden environments. She believes that as we bring our environments into balance we live happier and healthier lives, benefit all that we relate to, and help heal the earth.

Shelley is a senior disciple of His Holiness Grandmaster Lin Yun Rinpoche and Her Holiness Khadro Crystal Chu Rinpoche, leaders of Black Sect Tantric Buddhist Sect of Feng Shui. She has studied feng shui for more than eighteen years. She is a contributing author to, "Contemporary Earth Design, a Feng Shui Anthology" and has written articles for New Woman's Spirit Magazine, Feng Shui, the Journal, Landscape Architect and Specifier News and les nouvelles esthetiques. She has published *Keep Plants Healthy, Monthly Actions for Beautiful Gardens,* the first in a series of gardening guides. It is geared to the southern United States.

She teaches Feng Shui and Feng Shui landscape design principles for U.C.L.A. Extension and various other national venues. Shelley was a featured speaker for The Second International Feng Shui Conference and for the National Convention of the American Society of Landscape Architects 1997 and 1998 and the International Conference of Esthetics and Dermatology. Other venues where she has taught are California State College at Northridge, the Chicago Arboretum, Los Angeles Arboretum, Descanso Botanical Gardens, Long Island Institute of Feng Shui, California Landscape Contractors Association, The Learning Annex, the Beverly Hills Garden Show, South Coast Plaza Garden Show and Learning Tree University. Besides garden classes, she taught classes and workshops in Feng Shui, Feng Shui and Health, Prosperity Using Feng Shui, Feng Shui and Love, and Feng Shui for the Beauty Industry. She consulted on gardens, homes and corporations throughout the United States including Directtv headquarters in southern California.

She is a licensed as a Landscape Architect and has designed award winning residential landscapes. She has taught classes in landscape subjects including "The Garden As a Healing Space" and "Designing for Horticultural Therapy: Requirements for Successful Landscapes" for U.C.L.A. Extension and "How to Design Your Own Garden" for the Learning Annex.

Shelley was a guest star designer for the Home and Garden Network's "The Surprise Gardener" and filmed segments for local Los Angeles news shows. Shelley lectures, writes and works in Los Angeles. She does Feng Shui consultations for people's homes, businesses and gardens. She owns her own company, Harmony Gardens and can be reached through, (818) 505-9783 or her website, www.harmonygardens.net.

Acknowledgements

No one creates a book in a vacuum. I have received so much support from so many people to write this book. Of course my first thank you has to go to His Holiness Grandmaster Lin Yun Rinpoche whose guidance changed my life forever, Her Holiness Khadro Crystal Chu Rinpoche, who stepped into some mighty big shoes, and all the helpers at Yun Lin Temple. There were many eyes on my book as it was coming to fruition and wonderful suggestions and help from many. Thanks to Shena Huang, Katherine Metz, Linda Juratovac, Kathy Berrin, Elena Michaels, Marina Lighthouse, my editors Davida Rappaport, Jeanne McCafferty, and Christine LePorte. I am so grateful to my family, especially my husband who balances me by taking me out to play.

INDEX

References are to page numbers.

Terms presented in *italics* indicate names of plants and trees.